Laugharne in the Great War

Reflections 100 years on

Laugharne in the Great War

Reflections 100 years on

By
Talacharn Community History

Editors
Denize McIntyre & Peter Stopp

Copyright © 2018 Talacharn Community History

Published in 2018 by
Talacharn Community History

A CIP catalogue record for this book is
available from the British Library.

ISBN 978-1-9164968-0-4

Printed and bound in Wales by
Dinefwr Print & Design, Rawlings Road, Llandybie
Carmarthenshire, SA18 3YD

Contents

Rhagair

Dros y pedair blynedd ddiwethaf mae cymunedau ledled Cymru wedi bod yn cofio ac yn coffau aberth a chyfraniad eu cymunedau i'r Rhyfel Mawr. Nid yw Talacharn yn wahanol i leoliadau eraill yn hyn o beth ac mae ein cymdeithas hanes, Hanes Cymunedol Talacharn, wedi bod yn cymryd rhan mewn digwyddiadau a gweithgareddau lleol. Rydym ni wedi edrych ar effaith y Rhyfel ar ein cymuned; beth ddigwyddodd i bobl, beth wnaethon nhw a sut y bu i'r Rhyfel effeithio arnynt am flynyddoedd lawer wedi hynny. Roddem ni am i'n cymuned heddiw gofio, ac felly cawsom grant Cronfa Dreftadaeth y Loteri i'n helpu ni.

Mae ein tîm o wirfoddolwyr lleol wedi defnyddio'r grant hwn i ymchwilio a chofnodi atgofion, gwybodaeth ac eitemau personol lleol. Rydym ni wedi gweithio gyda'n hysgol gynradd, wedi creu adnoddau y gall ysgolion eraill eu defnyddio, cynnal tair arddangosfa, cyflwyno sgyrsiau, creu cofnodion, ychwanegu ffotograffau Gasgliad y Bobl ar lein a chynhyrchu erthyglau yn ein papur bro lleol. Helpodd y tudalennau yng Nghylchlythyr Talacharn symbylu rhai ymatebion a daeth tameidiau o wybodaeth i law gan unigolion yn y gymuned, a ddatgelodd straeon, o'u cyfuno, yr oedd modd i ni eu rhannu.

Y tîm ysgrifennu oedd: Denize McIntyre (cyd-olygydd); Zoe Gray; Chris Delaney; Janet Bradshaw; Steven John; Raymond Edwards; Jeff Watts a Peter Stopp (cyd-olygydd). Tynnodd y Prosiect ar wybodaeth, straeon, dogfennau ffotograffau a chymorth gan nifer fawr o bobl, ac ni fyddai'r llyfr hwn wedi bod yn bosib hebddynt. Yn eu plith y mae: Rosemary a Wil Rees; Ketura Rhodes; Emma McGrigor; Harcourt John; John Bradshaw; Ruth Roberts; Heulwen a Bob Elward; Brian Reynolds; Keith a Wendy Edwards; Kimberley Perry; Dyfrig Dafis; Charles ac Ann Deschoolmeester; Mavis Deschoolmeester; Robert Wright; Picton Gibbin; Christophe Declercq; Peter Boyle; James Meek; y Tad Chris Lewis-Jenkins; Glenn Davies; Roy Thomas; Jackie Griffith; Jean Anderson; Doreen Lewis; Paul Pearce; Iris John; Alice Pyper; Greg Lewis; Felicity Boyce; Elsa Davies; George a Julia Phillips; Seimon Pugh Jones; Andy Edwards;

Margaret Hatfield; Roger Thomas; Raymond Bowen; a Cathryn Elward. Rydym ni'n eithriadol ddiolchgar i bawb sydd wedi ein cynorthwyo a gobeithio y byddan nhw'n teimlo fod y gyfrol hon yn ganlyniad teilwng o'u cefnogaeth.

Rydym ni wedi defnyddio'r gwasanaethau rhagorol canlynol yn helaeth: Llyfrgell Gyfeiriadol Caerfyrddin; Gwasanaeth Archif Sir Gaerfyrddin; Amgueddfa Sir Gaerfyrddin; a Llyfrgell Genedlaethol Cymru. Cawsom fenthyg y rhan fwyaf o'r lluniau gan bobl leol garedig. Rydym wedi ceisio sefydlu ffynhonnell pob un ohonynt, ac rydym wedi cael trwyddedau a chaniatâd gan yr Amgueddfa Ryfel Ymerodrol a'r Archif Genedlaethol Brydeinig i ddefnyddio rhai darluniau. Rydym ni'n ddiolchgar am yr adnoddau a ddarparwyd gan y gwasanaethau hyn, sy'n cyfoethogi'r gyfrol o ran gwybodaeth a darluniau.

Rydym hefyd wedi pwyso ar – ond heb geisio dyblygu – llyfr Steve John: *A Town in Mourning,* sy'n coffau'r holl ddynion o Dalacharn a gofir ar y Gofeb sydd y tu allan i Neuadd Goffa Talacharn. Adroddir hanes y Rhyfel yn dda mewn llyfrau niferus ac nid yw'n cael ei hailadrodd yma, heblaw am roi straeon Talacharn yn eu cyd-destun. Roeddem ni eisiau rhoi rhyw gymaint o bwyslais ar sut brofiad oedd hi i bobl oedd gartref yn Nhalacharn pa effaith gafodd y Rhyfel arnyn nhw? Profodd hyn i fod yn fwy o her. Mae cenhedlaeth y Rhyfel wedi mynd ac aeth gormod o amser heibio er mwyn cael gwybodaeth uniongyrchol gan y rheiny oedd yn fyw bryd hynny. Oherwydd yr erchyllterau a wynebwyd gan bobl fu'n byw drwyddynt yn ystod y Rhyfel roedd hi'n anodd gan lawer fu'n cymryd rhan i siarad am eu profiadau o gwbl. Bu'n rhaid cael gwybodaeth yn anuniongyrchol drwy gyfrwng straeon cyfoes mewn papurau newydd a chan yr ychydig drigolion a allai gofio straeon a adroddwyd iddynt gan eu rhieni a'u rhieni hwythau.

Yr hyn sy'n dod i'r amlwg drwy gyfrwng y straeon a'r atgofion yw ymdeimlad fod y rhan fwyaf o bobl yn ei theimlo'n ddyletswydd i gefnogi'r Rhyfel. Gwnaethant hynny â stoiciaeth yn wyneb y cyfan a daflwyd atynt ganddo. Efallai y byddai pobl heddiw wedi gwingo rhag ymwneud mor barod â rhyfela. Efallai mai dyma un o ganlyniadau cadarnhaol y rhyfel a ddaeth i'r amlwg gennym. Er ei bod hi'n amser maith ers diwedd y rhyfel, erys elfennau yn ein bywydau hyd heddiw sy'n ganlyniad uniongyrchol i'r Rhyfel a ddaeth i ben gan mlynedd yn ôl.

Yn y gyfrol hon rydym ni'n archwilio straeon y rheiny wnaeth fyw drwy'r rhyfel mewn brwydr ac yn y cartref. Byddwch chi'n gweld sut effeithiwyd ar bobl leol gan y rhyfel ac yn darganfod straeon am bobl gyffredin yn gwneud pethau anghyffredin iawn. Newidiwyd cymdeithas gan y Rhyfel mewn ffyrdd y gellir eu teimlo hyd heddiw. Rydym ni wedi cyhoeddi'r gyfrol hon ar gyfer y gymuned fel cofnod o'r hyn a ddysgwyd gan bob un ohono ac i gofio'n annwyl am genedlaethau'r gorffennol.

Preface

For the last four years communities across Wales have been commemorating and remembering the sacrifices and contributions their community made during the Great War. Laugharne is no exception and our history society, *Talacharn Community History*, has been involved in local events and activities. We have looked at the impact of the war on our community; what happened to people, what they did and how it affected them for many years afterwards. We wanted our community today to remember, and obtained a Heritage Lottery Fund grant to help us.

Our team of local volunteers have used this grant to research and record local recollections, information and artefacts. We have worked with our local primary school, generated resources for other schools to use, held three exhibitions, given talks, created records, added photographs to the online *People's Collection Wales* and produced articles in our monthly community publication. The Laugharne Newsletter pages helped to stimulate some responses, and snippets of information came in from individuals in the community which often, when combined, revealed stories we could share.

The writing team comprised: Denize McIntyre (Co-editor); Zoe Gray; Chris Delaney; Janet Bradshaw; Steven John; Raymond Edwards; Jeff Watts and Peter Stopp (Co-editor). The project drew on information, anecdotes, documents, photographs and help from a large number of people, without whom this book would not have been possible. They include: Rosemary and Wil Rees; Ketura Rhodes; Emma McGrigor; Harcourt John; John Bradshaw; Ruth Roberts; Heulwen and Bob Elward; Brian Reynolds; Keith and Wendy Edwards; Kimberley Perry; Dyfrig Dafis; Charles and Ann Deschoolmeester; Mavis Deschoolmeester; Robert Wright; Picton Gibbin; Christophe Declercq; Peter Boyle; James Meek; Father Chris Lewis-Jenkins; Glenn Davies; Roy Thomas; Jackie Griffith; Jean Anderson; Doreen Lewis; Paul Pearce; Iris John; Alice Pyper; Greg Lewis; Felicity Boyce; Elsa Davies; George and Julia Phillips;

Seimon Pugh Jones; Andy Edwards; Margaret Hatfield; Roger Thomas; Raymond Bowen; and Cathryn Elward. If we have omitted a name from our thanks, then it is simply because of our fallibility but be assured that we are really thankful for your input. We are extremely grateful to all those who helped and we hope that they feel this book is a worthy outcome for their support.

We have made extensive use of the excellent services of Carmarthen Reference Library; Carmarthenshire Archives Service; Carmarthenshire County Museum; and the National Library of Wales. Most of the photographs have been kindly loaned by local people. We have tried to establish the sources of all of them and we have obtained permission licences from the Imperial War Museum and National Archives to use certain illustrations. We are grateful for the resources provided by these services, which enrich the book with both information and illustrations.

We have also drawn on, but tried not to duplicate, Steve John's book *A Township in Mourning*, which remembers all those men from Laugharne who died and are commemorated on the memorial outside Laugharne's Memorial Hall. The history of the war is told well in numerous books and is not retold here, other than to put Laugharne's stories into context. We wanted to place some emphasis on what it was like for people at home in Laugharne, what was the effect of the war on them? This proved more difficult. The war generation has gone and too much time has passed to be able to get direct information from those who were alive then. The horrors they lived through meant that most of those engaged in it could not bring themselves to speak of it at all. Information had to come indirectly through contemporary newspaper accounts and from the few people who could recall anecdotes passed on to them from their parents and grandparents.

What comes through those accounts and recollections is a sense that most people saw it as their duty to support the war. They did so with a stoicism in the face of all that it threw at them. Perhaps people today would shy away from engaging so readily in war. Perhaps this was one of the positive outcomes of the war we have identified. Although it is long past, there are elements that remain in our lives today that still owe their origins to the war that ended a hundred years ago.

In this book we explore the stories of those who lived through the war in battle and at home. You will find out how the war affected local people and discover stories of ordinary people doing extraordinary things. The war changed society in ways that can still be felt today. We have published this book for the community as a record of what we have all learnt and to cherish the memory of previous generations.

Prologue

Life in Laugharne prior to the War

Laugharne harbour in the 1900s.

In the years leading up to the First World War life was so different from today that it is difficult now for our imaginations to accurately capture the realities of those years. In the eighteenth and early nineteenth centuries Laugharne had been a thriving port and commercial town. But the arrival of the railway to St Clears led to the shift of trade there, so by the start of the twentieth century the port trade had largely died away. The majority of the young men in Laugharne were manual workers. Some worked in the fishing and cockling industries, as did some women, although most young women worked in domestic service.

The decline in local job opportunities had led to a large number of men moving away to work in the coal mines of the Amman Valley, Llanelli and the

Rhondda. Others had moved even further afield, to start new lives in the Dominions of Canada, Australia, South Africa and New Zealand. For a few the connection with the sea lingered on as they joined the merchant navy, whilst for others the army may have presented a more secure living and an escape from poverty.

> **Individual shops and trades in Laugharne, 1914:**
> *Coal Dealer; Corn & Flour merchant; Draper; Builder; Miller; Insurance Agent; Grocer; Cockle Dealer; Tailor; Fishmonger; Bootmaker; Confectioner; Builder's merchant; Chemist & Post Office; Cycle dealer; Monumental Mason; Bus & Taxi service.*

The Township still possessed a large number of shops and small businesses, which opened six days a week until late in the evening. They included 12 general shops, four butchers, two bakers, blacksmiths, builders and banks plus 17 others listed in *Kelly's Directory* for 1914 (see panel). And, of course, public houses – of which there were 10 – open all hours! It even had a cinema, although this closed temporarily at the end of July whilst electric lighting was installed. Most needs were therefore catered for within the Township. It meant that people shopped and socialised within the community, and so developed a strong sense of community fellowship. It is possible to gain some sense of the times by looking at the lives of a few individuals, and these people will appear again later in this book.

The splendid Georgian-fronted houses in King Street were occupied by those on a good income. Among the better-off families was that of Colonel and Mary Bolton. Mary raised her two sons, John 'Ritso' and Stuart Bladen, in Laugharne, living in her aunt Federata Leach's Elm House, on King Street. Having inherited the house from their aunt when she died in 1913 they settled permanently there. The boys went to private boarding schools so were often away but returned to Laugharne for holidays and entered fully into Laugharne life.

Ritso was popular among the young people in Laugharne. He was educated at Suffolk Hall, Cheltenham; Pelham House, Folkestone; and Bedford Grammar School, where he was elected Head Boy. In 1912 he won a place at the Royal Military Academy at Woolwich, and in August 1914 was gazetted as a Lieu-tenant in the Royal Field Artillery, serving in the 104th Battery, 22nd Brigade, which returned from India in August 1914 to join the 7th Division. He came home on leave in July, 1914 for his 21st birthday party and his popularity is

Ritso Bolton.

Carmarthen Journal and *South Wales Advertiser*: 31st July 1914:

We extend our hearty congratulations to Mr Ritso Bolton on attaining his majority on 24th inst. Master Ritso, as he is familiarly and affectionately styled, is the eldest son of Colonel and Mrs Bolton, Elm House, who to cele-brate the coming of age presented their heir with an attractive and powerful motor-car. Mr Bolton is a very popular young man and his occasional home-coming is anticipated with pleasure by his numerous friends, old and young, rich and poor alike, for he knows them all, and has a hearty handshake and kindly word for everyone, and little wonder that the parish church bells pealed merrily at midday in his honour. He has had a successful and distinguished scholastic career and ere long enters the Army. Good luck to you, sir.

evident from the fact that church bells were rung to commemorate the day and the report (see panel) in the local press gushed effusively.

Another resident of King Street was Robert Henry Tyler, Laugharne's schoolteacher throughout the war. He had been born in Carmarthen around 1874, one of seven children. At age 17 he became a 'pupil teacher' from which he graduated to become Laugharne's teacher by 1901, when he was boarding with the blacksmith, Thomas Jones, and his family in Victoria Street. By 1911, however, he had moved into Osborne House on King Street with his widower father, Samuel. We know nothing more of his early life, but the fact that his sister was named Florence Nightingale Tyler, and one of his brothers Garibaldi Tyler, suggests an element of family admiration for national heroes or uniforms!

He took an active part in Laugharne life, for example through support of the Rugby Club. Perhaps Mr Tyler's admiration for the military also led to him founding, in 1910, one of the first scout troops in Wales. They are pictured in 1911, in front of his house. Mr Tyler is on the left, and Mr Ladd (Assistant Scoutmaster) on the right. The Rev. F. Atterbury-Thomas has joined them and quite a crowd seems to have gathered for the occasion.

Mr Tyler (left) and the scout troop outside Mr Tyler's home: Osborne House.

William Constable.

William Constable in London.

At each end of the town lived the poorer people, such as the Constable family, in Horsepool Road. William Constable, shown here in his scout uniform, was born in 1898, the middle child of five living with their mother, Jane, who earned some income as a dressmaker, and their grandmother, Bridget. William's father, Philip, was an engineer on chartered sea vessels operating out of Llanelli and so spent much of his time away. Soon after leaving school William had escaped to London to work in a gentleman's outfitters, from where he sent the photograph of himself. He was happy there, describing in a letter home that life there was 'much more to his liking'.

At the other end of town, Frog Street and Gosport were where the seafolk – cocklers and fishermen – lived and shopped locally in Thomas's grocery shop at the bottom of Gosport. Even further away, beyond Water Street and The Lacques, past the long-deserted tucking mills, were families such as the Lewis family whom we shall encounter in more detail in Chapter 3.

Perched high around the town, each enjoying magnificent views over the estuary, were the houses of wealthier families, those of independent means. To the west was Fernhill, home of the Hurt Peel family; to the east Glanymor was occupied by the Falkeners; further south, beyond Broadway lay Broadway Mansion, recent new home of the Eccles; and to the north was Mapsland occupied by Miss Cunningham, and The Glen by Commander Brayshay.

Further out lay farms, such as Honeycorse near Coygan, overlooking Laugharne Marsh, and home to Raymond Morse who also owned and managed the quarry there. As a rural, agricultural community Laugharne was, to some extent, self-sufficient – the surrounding farms, being a mixture of dairy, livestock and arable. Kelly's Post Office Directory for South Wales lists over 40 farmers and their farms in the district in 1910. There was a local milk factory in Broadway, as well as the butchers, bakers, and a corn and flour merchant in the town, supplying grain to the farmers, flour to the bakers and maize for feeding poultry. Many people would have kept their own chickens and grown a few vegetables and some would have kept their own pig. And, of course, there was direct access to the sea and fish, together with a thriving cockle industry; both fish and cockles being sold door to door by local hawkers.

Unlike today when our national newspapers and magazines give prominence to the daily lives of entertainers and media stars, reporting their movements and activities in detail, in those days such people were still regarded dubiously, as of doubtful morals. Instead, both national and local papers reported the movements and activities of local society leaders – those people of 'independent means' and their families. This included, locally, Mr Eccles; the

Boltons and Hurt Peels. Also, whereas today any scandals committed by such prominent people do (eventually, at least) get reported, a hundred years ago they were more likely to be hushed up, so we mostly get only positive news of their lives. For example, when Mr Peel committed suicide, shooting himself in the drive of Fernhill in 1905, it was reported locally simply as a sad death, with no mention of suicide. On the other hand, the lives of the poor were, much as today, only reported when they broke the law or caused some other offence! So looking back at the press we get a somewhat distorted picture of the times.

When Mary Curtis wrote her history of Laugharne, 40 years earlier, Laugharne society then was very clearly divided between the better-off gentlefolk and the labouring classes. That distinction still held to a great extent by the start of the war. People seemed to accept their allotted stations in life, so forelocks were still tugged and women even curtsied as members of Laugharne's upper-classes rode by.

Services that are taken for granted today – electricity, tapwater, flush toilets – were, of course, all non-existent. The water supply was from various pumps in the town: at the Croft on Clifton Street, Eynon's Down, at the Pump House on Holloway Road and opposite Lacques Cottage on Water Street. For lighting people used gas lighting, paraffin lamps or candles. Travel was still by horse-drawn carriages or carts, though the railway was popular for longer journeys. Since journeys could be onerous most people did not travel far, hence Laugharne being full of those shops and services.

Miss Ethel Falkener and companion out for a ride.

Before the war there were few employment opportunities for women here. The two main ones were cockling and domestic service. Cockling was clearly hard, back-bending, cold, wet work at all hours dictated by the tides. But domestic service was also very onerous. The 1911 Census reveals that in the 23 occupied dwellings in King Street more than half had at least one domestic servant.

One former domestic servant recollected her day starting at 6am to prepare breakfast, then housework until 11am when she went to the kitchen to prepare lunch, followed by more housework – dusting, cleaning, polishing, washing, ironing – through to 9pm when she went to bed. She recalled one evening when at about 10pm the duty bell woke her. She got out of bed, dressed and went to see what was wanted, to be told, "Draw the curtains to, it's getting rather dark outside"!

Another tale, from a local resident, of her time in domestic service illustrates how strictly rules of dress code were applied. Housemaids could be expected, as she was, to change after lunch from their morning costume to the afternoon one. Early one afternoon she was descending the main staircase towards the hall when the front door opened and in came the owners. The maid was so alarmed because she was still wearing her morning uniform that she leaped through the landing window into the garden outside simply to escape being spotted so inappropriately dressed!

Workers in domestic service not only worked long hours each working day but had only one or, at most, two afternoons a week as free time. Because board and keep were provided the salary could be tiny, too. And some employers could be very hard task mistresses. Miss Falkener, for example, would insist that furniture was polished afresh and to check it was so she would pour water onto the table surface. So the opportunities of alternative work that opened up later during the war years understandably saw a number of workers escaping domestic service drudgery even, as we shall see, to go into dangerous work such as the munitions factory at Pembrey.

A significant difference between now and then was that in the years leading up to and during the war Laugharne's St Martin's church and local chapels played a large role in people's lives. That most people attended one of them every Sunday, is evident from the fact that when the Government wanted to make an announcement it did so in the traditional way: by sending a letter to every church across the nation to be read out in the Sunday services. Laugharne was no exception, even the church choir was strong in numbers. So the regular services held later to remember the local fallen served to remind everyone of the horrors of war and of their losses. These services, whether it was family or friends, drew even larger congregation numbers than usual.

During the days leading up to the Declaration of War, life in Laugharne was relatively idyllic. Local agricultural shows were planned around the county for July and August and notices announced a new dining hall at the Beach Hotel at Pendine. The Annual Laugharne Regatta and Carnival was held on 3rd August, 1914 and a concert was held in the grounds of the castle, where the Pembroke Dock Military Band played to the massed crowd. Local bus companies also advertised day trips to Lampeter, Tenby, Aberystwyth, Pembroke, and Pembroke Dock. So during the first three days of August 1914 enlisting into and fighting with the armed forces was obviously far from the minds of local men and women.

Chapter 1

The Great War and the Call to Arms

WHY WAR?

To start this exploration of Laugharne's Great War experience it just makes sense to ask 'Why war? And why now?' since everything else – the story of the Township, its response to the situation, and the experiences of its people – follows on from the Declaration of War made by the British Government on Tuesday, 4th August, 1914.

Many people believe that the First World War was started when Archduke Franz Ferdinand, the heir presumptive of the Austro-Hungarian Empire, was shot and killed while he and his wife were on an official visit to Sarajevo, the capital of Bosnia (which was then in the south east corner of the Empire). This obviously is not entirely wrong, but that deadly event was more like a fuse which set off the dormant, but very fragile, time bomb which was the state of international relations at that time. It is almost certainly the case that the war would have happened anyway: if it had not been triggered by this assassination, then it would have been some other matter. Just a matter of time.

So what did people in Laugharne understand about the international situation? What information did they get in the period leading up to events in Sarajevo? Did the Declaration of War in August come as a complete shock or was it, to a degree, somewhat expected?

The first thing to realise about feelings at the time was that many, if not all, of the major countries of Europe were very strongly nationalistic. There was, certainly in the UK, Germany, Austria-Hungary, Italy, France and Russia, a belief that their country was the best, strongest, most impressive and respected – and these attitudes made national leaders and politicians aggressive and assertive in their dealings with others. Keeping on good terms with the neighbours just was not seen to be a high priority when one's view of one's own country was so high, and of the neighbour – so low. This 'jingoism' was rife throughout the press at the time. It was not arrogance on the part of individuals; it was a general national feeling across a number of key countries and it pervaded the British daily newspapers.

Imperialism, the possession of an empire, was another issue. Britain had a vast empire which was a source of enormous wealth and prestige. France, too, had built itself an empire concentrating chiefly in Africa and South East Asia. Germany wanted an empire, to gain the same advantages and status that other countries with empires had, and it set about getting one through colonising areas of Africa and, later, annexing parts of France and Belgium.

In addition, Laugharne's people would have been familiar with the build-up of tensions in Europe caused by the system of 'alliances': groups of countries which had come together with binding promises to support each other if one country had a quarrel with another from the *opposing* alliance. These alliances went back a long way before 1914. As early as 1839 Britain had been a signatory to a treaty to protect Belgium.

All national newspapers, and other popular reading material such as 'Punch' magazine, regularly covered the political goings-on and, just as today, there was expert discussion about what this meant and whether, for example, trade would be affected, or whether conflict would follow.

In 1882, Germany, Austria-Hungary and Italy formed the 'Triple Alliance'. This arrangement set alarm bells ringing for France, Britain and Russia and, after much discussion, political manoeuvrings and hand-wringing, by 1907 these three joined together to become the 'Triple Entente'. The cartoon, showing a Peace figure 'intruding' in discussions between the Emperor of Germany and the Russian Czar comes from July 1888 – revealing that there was, even then, some scepticism that peace would figure in their talks.

So, seven years or more before the assassination in Sarajevo, Europe was divided firmly into two opposing camps. Each camp was deeply suspicious of the other, and throughout these years the politicians and military leaders watched, waited, planned and committed to help each other *if* there was a war.

As if these two groups of nationalistically-minded countries was not risky enough, many of them were also engaged in an arms race. Germany and Britain were in competition to build bigger and deadlier warships; a rivalry which dated back to the last decade of the century before! For example, the widely-read

OUR "MUTUAL FRIEND."

Spirit of Peace (to the two Emperors). "HOPE I DON'T INTRUDE!!!"

Punch Magazine's sceptical cartoon, July 1888.

Daily Express in 1906 carried a front page story with the headline 'World's Greatest Battleship' referring to the launch of the new HMS Dreadnought. Newspaper coverage like this would have prompted lots of discussion, pride and patriotism here in Laugharne, and around the country, but it was actually an arms race that was rushing wildly toward conflict.

So, in a nutshell, there were wealthy countries with an inflated sense of their own might, the military means to wage a large-scale war, massive ambitions for empires and, most dangerously, a set of alliances/agreements which meant that as soon as one ally in a group was threatened then the combined forces of all partners came in behind them. There would be no backing out. The agreements of the two groups were as if written in stone, and they were

3

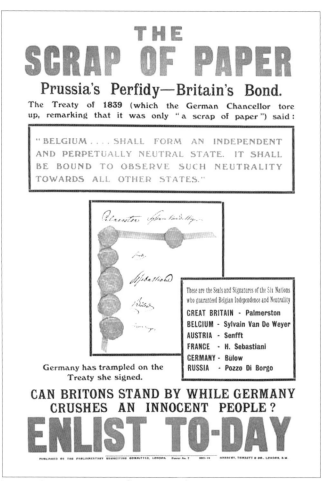

THE SCRAP OF PAPER: Depicting the Treaty of London, signed on 19th April, 1839,
by Britain, France, Russia, Austria and Germany, the treaty guaranteed the existence,
neutrality and sovereignty of the newly recognised country of Belgium.

dangerous. As soon as Austria-Hungary declared war on Serbia (as a result of that event in Sarajevo) the two sets of allies became belligerent and shouting. Patriotism and indignation kicked in, the obligations in the treaties came into operation and Europe was, inevitably, at war.

So, were the folk of Laugharne in 1914 shocked when war broke out? In all probability, they were not and, even more significantly, most people probably felt it was worth it. They were imbued with the idea that Britain was the greatest so a positive result would be achieved in a very short while. What they could not know then, of course, was that it would drag on for over four long, miserable years, cost around 18 million lives, and that the lives of few people here would ever be the same again.

4

RECRUITMENT

Following the Declaration of War by the British Government on 4th August, 1914, triggered by the assassination of Archduke Franz Ferdinand a week earlier, a prepared war machine moved smoothly into action. As well as advertising for recruits in local newspapers, posters were pasted on walls around the county asking for both the army and navy reservists and for territorial and yeomanry soldiers to mobilise and re-join their units. Instead of the expected panic, complacency about the enormity of the events in Europe meant that life still carried on as normal. For now the general public in Laugharne and its surrounding area did not feel a need to enlist, as it was widely believed that if Britain and Germany went to war the conflict would be over by Christmas. This was a somewhat different trend to the country as a whole where, following a relatively slow start, there was a sudden surge in recruiting in late August and early September 1914, with almost 480,000 enlistments by 12th September.

There was already a small number of local men serving in the armed forces in the months prior to the outbreak of war. They included: Hugh Lewis John, of Soland Gate (St Clears), serving in India with the 1st Welsh; Charles Vincent Todman had enlisted into the London Regiment (TA) on 16th April, 1914; John Arloe Edward Thomas had been in the Royal Navy since 9th September, 1902; and George Lewis since 26th December, 1899. Several others, including William Neville Hurt Peel and William Fuller, were army reservists who had previously served in the army but had left to take up civilian occupations. Another young man from Laugharne, Eric Western Wilson, had just gained a commission into the 2nd Battalion, Royal Inniskilling Fusiliers. Lieutenant Morgan Grainger Jones, of Llanmiloe House, was serving with the Royal Welsh Fusiliers. Captain Price Vaughan Lewes, CBE, DSO, of the Royal Navy, was on holiday in Laugharne with his wife, while Major George Fison Muller, of the Royal Marines, and his wife Katherine, were making their way to Laugharne for a holiday with his Aunt, Mrs Fanny Brayshay, at the Glen.

Including the number of local men serving with the Merchant Navy just prior to the outbreak of the Great War, it is obvious that the Township was relatively well represented in the armed forces. But the outbreak of war would soon see recruitment levels on a scale never experienced anywhere before, let alone in sleepy Laugharne.

Lord Kitchener, the new Secretary of State for War, considered the pre-war Territorial Army to be untrained and ineffective and therefore he launched his famous 'call to arms' for men to enlist.

The famous recruiting poster depicting Lord Horatio Kitchener:
'Your Country Needs You'

To organise recruitment in West Wales it was decided that Carmarthenshire and Pembrokeshire would fall under the 41st Recruiting District with Carmarthen and Llanelli as the main recruiting centres. Recruits at local towns and villages were to be sent to either of these to attest.

Laugharne men who were, by then, domiciled in Dominion countries such as Canada, Australia and New Zealand, were among the first to enlist in their armed forces. Commander Joseph Hamilton Arthur Beresford was already serving with the Royal Australian Navy, while George Watts, David Thomas John, James Picton Davies, Evan Benjamin Thomas and Robert Craig David were early enlistees into the Australian Imperial Force. Percy Leonard Sampson, an army pensioner who had worked as a servant at Island House, and John Edward Price, late of the Brown's Hotel, were among the first from Laugharne to enlist into the Canadian Expeditionary Force. Colonel Arthur Heely Bolton was already serving with the Indian Army, whilst Gwynne Clayton Brewer was an early enlistee into the New Zealand Expeditionary Force.

In Laugharne, young men had several options for which unit in which to enlist. For example, Carmarthen was home to 'E' Company of the 4th (Territorial) Battalion, Welsh Regiment, stationed at Picton Terrace, along with 'C' Squadron of the Pembroke Yeomanry. These territorial and yeomanry battalions were formed of local men, some of whom had fought with the Imperial Yeomanry or the Welch Regiment during the South African War of 1899-1902 and they attended regular training camps around Wales after the formation of the Territorial Force in 1908. Whilst the requirements to join the 4th Welsh were minimal, yeomanry volunteers had to provide their own horses, thus were usually more well-off men or sons of landowners. These units held regular parades in Carmarthen, usually culminating in their assembly in Carmarthen Park, where their bands would play on the bandstand to throngs of sightseers and well-wishers.

Military parades: a parade of local members of the Pembroke Yeomanry in Carmarthen Park c1913.

The majority of officers at the outbreak of war were from the upper classes of local society, and many were prominent landowners, such as the Campbells of Stackpole and Golden Grove, and the Philipps family of Picton Castle and Manorbier, who were well known throughout West Wales. The Great War would have a profound effect on the upper classes in the years after the armistice, with several local estates left intestate due to the heirs being killed in action.

Lord Kensington, former Lord of the Manor of Llandawke, Commanding Officer of Welsh Horse Yeomanry and later the 25th Battalion, Royal Welsh Fusiliers.

Prominent landowner families with ties to Laugharne were: Lord Kensington, who counted Llandawke Manor among his many homes, and Morgan Jones of Llanmiloe. In the Township itself lived the Hurt-Peels of Fern Hill, the Mordaunt-Smiths of Milton Bank, the Western Wilsons of The Cors, the Falkeners of Glan-y-Môr, and Herbert Eccles of Broadway Mansion. All these families, apart from the Falkeners, saw sons and nephews go off to war, some never to return, while many of their daughters and wives volunteered to serve as nurses and orderlies.

Within days of the Declaration of War the reservists from Laugharne re-joined their old regiments. They included William Charles Fuller, now living in Swansea, who re-joined the 2nd Battalion, Welsh Regiment at Cardiff. Hugh Lewis John re-joined the 1st Battalion, South Wales Borderers in Brecon. Thomas Lewis Ebsworth, of The Beach Hotel, Pendine, who had previously served with the Royal Engineers, joined the 6th Welsh (TA). Lewis Rees re-joined the Royal Engineers at Wakefield. Major Claude Vyvian Congreve, of Island House, also re-joined his old regiment from retirement. By the end of August the other Laugharne men who enlisted were: Cyril Frederick Lanning, who enlisted from school into the 16th Battalion, London Regiment; Frank Roberts enlisted at Preston into the Royal Field Artillery; and Martyn Tulloch Vaughan Lewes left his parents holidaying at Laugharne to enlist into the Welsh Regiment. His father, Pryse Vaughan Lewes also left Laugharne for Portsmouth to take command of the battleship, HMS Superb; while Major George Fison Muller, upon receiving a telegram notifying him of his recall, re-joined the Royal Marine Light Infantry at Portsmouth.

*The men of the 2nd Welsh entraining at Pembroke Dock to begin their move
to the front with the British Expeditionary Force.*

Several men from Laugharne appear to have been among the original enlistees into either the 4th Welsh or the Pembroke Yeomanry. Among those members of the 4th Welsh were: Thomas Morgan, Frederick James Renfrey, William Ivor Evans, and William Killa. Only a very few served with the Pembroke Yeomanry, two of whom were George Brown and Henry Lewis Bevan, while Daniel Davies of Broadway, and Thomas Morgan were reported to have enlisted into the regiment in August. Many more would follow as the war advanced.

At least twenty women from Laugharne would serve during the war. Their role will be explored further in chapter 6. Amongst those known to have served with the British Red Cross and Queen Alexandra's Imperial Military Nursing Service were: Catherine Allen; Ruth Laugharne Allen; Constance Elizabeth David; Mary Hopla David; Penelope Davies; Emily Myfanwy Jones; Eileen Mordaunt-Smith; Dulcie Hurt Peel; Janet Ravenscroft Starke; Jane Maud Todman; Margery Lilian Todman; and Matilda Thomasina Todman. With the Women's Army Auxiliary Corps served Annie Beale (née Davies); Elsie Mary Brown; Jane Brown; Moddey Brown; Miss A. Davies, Cornelia Evans, Miss L. Phillips and Miss Bertha Williams. Minnie Hurt Peel of Fern Hill and Mrs Morgan Jones of Llanmiloe House also gave up countless hours for fund raising and helping the war effort in any way they could, as shall be seen in chapter 2.

9

Among the first of the Laugharne soldiers in France were Ben Garside Turpin and Eric Western Wilson, while William Thomas, of Kingaddle, was a reservist who joined the British Expeditionary Force (the BEF) two weeks after it first arrived. Many of the local men serving at this early stage of the war were with the 2nd Battalion, Welsh Regiment. News of the actions in which this regiment, and local men in particular, were engaged would have been eagerly awaited by folks at home, and it is very likely that this news acted as a further stimulus to recruitment – even the news that Eric Western Wilson was the first Laugharne man to make the ultimate sacrifice. He was 21 years old and the flag on the ancient church of St Martin's was lowered to half-mast for the first of what proved to be many times.

A recruitment drive in Carmarthenshire, carried out by officers of the newly formed Welsh Horse Yeomanry, resulted in several men from Laugharne joining this new regiment. John Davies, an army reservist who had re-joined the South Wales Borderers at Brecon, deserted in order to join the Welsh Horse. William Dearing, a gamekeeper at Llanmiloe House, Gordon Hoare (the son of PC Hoare), and Frank McDonald, a farm worker at Hugdon, all enlisted into the regiment soon after its formation. Amongst its officers was Lieutenant John Garbutt Hutchinson, of Claradine House, Pendine, and the regiment was commanded by the 6th Baron Kensington, Hugh Edwardes, a prominent Pembrokeshire landowner, who had fought in the Boer War, and whose family had once owned the Castle Lloyd, Westmead and Llanmiloe estates.

On 3rd September several of the local newspapers carried another urgent call for recruits:

> The appeal now being made in West Wales for recruits for Lord Kitchener's Army ought to meet with a ready response in the two counties of the 41st Area (Pembrokeshire and Carmarthenshire). Recruiting offices have been opened in some of the more populous centres, with Llanelly as headquarters and young men desirous of offering their services to their country at this critical juncture cannot do better than make application without delay. A soldier cannot be trained in a day and Lord Kitchener is anxious that all recruits should make themselves efficient with as little delay as possible. It is important, therefore, that prompt application should be made.

With this expansion of the new army, a growing political force in Wales led by the Chancellor, David Lloyd George, envisioned the creation of a specific

Welsh Army Corps. A patriotic speech at the Queen's Hall, London, on 19th September, 1914, laid the foundations for the formation of its Executive Committee. The dream was to raise a Welsh Army Corps consisting of two divisions, which would take to the field together. The new Executive Committee was aware that many Welshmen had already been recruited, but it was soon clear that raising sufficient men for an Army Corps for Wales would take a lot of hard work. Nonetheless, the first stages of recruiting the men had begun and between 40,000 and 50,000 additional men were sought.

Carmarthenshire was estimated to have just over 26,000 men of military age, ranging from 20 to 40 years old. The Carmarthenshire County Committee was formed to draw from this group of men the numbers not only required to raise a new infantry battalion, but also enough men to supply reinforcements to this battalion as well as to the regular and territorial armies.

Over the coming months the first part of the dream of a Welsh Army Corps became reality with the formation of the 43rd (Welsh) Division [later renumbered the 38th]. Part of this new division was the 15th (Service) Battalion Welsh Regiment under the title of 'The Carmarthenshire Battalion'.

The Chancellor of the Exchequer, David Lloyd George.
He lived for a while in Pembrokeshire and later became
Prime Minister of Great Britain, helping guide
the country to victory over Germany.

A platoon of the 15th Welsh Regiment on the sands at Rhyl.

Whilst the recruitment drive in Carmarthenshire was being widely advertised in the press and driven by local dignitaries, the need for food production was also in the thoughts of the authorities. The *Carmarthen Journal* of 18th September noted the need for recruits, comparing the passion being felt in the colonies to aid the Mother Country. It also described the importance of farming in this great time of crisis. There was, therefore, something of a conflict between the need for men in the armed forces and in food production – one that would continue throughout the war.

At a major meeting at Carmarthen on 18th September, attended by all county dignitaries, the question of patriotism was raised and further calls to arms were made to the county's manpower. The same edition of *The Journal* controversially reported the poor numbers of recruits from the non-conformist section of the county, stating that:

> Welshmen leave it to the English church-goer to fight their war for them while they sit at home and sing *'Hen Wlad fy Nhadau'* and listen to sermons on the wickedness of the war!

Further scorn was placed on the Welshmen of Carmarthenshire in an open letter, printed in the *Carmarthen Journal*, sent by Major Delmé Davies-Evans. The officer wrote of his dismay upon completing the administration of the attestation papers of the Pembroke Yeomanry when he realised that the majority of its men who had volunteered for overseas service were English-born lads who had been working on farms in West Wales! Davies-Evans openly accused the farmers of West Wales of cowardice, thus causing fury in his home county. The newspaper itself regarded the lack of enthusiasm of Welsh farmers as being purely a case of ignorance of the dangers facing the country.

Major Delmé Davies-Evans, second in command of the Pembroke Yeomanry. A prominent figure in Carmarthenshire. He later commanded the 2/8th Battalion Worcestershire Regiment. Following the war he unveiled several local war memorials, including that at St Clears.

Laugharne resident, Herbert Eccles of Broadway Mansion, was the owner of the Briton Ferry Steelworks. After a spread of socialist anti-war rhetoric at Port Talbot, Eccles attempted to quell the socialist upsurge and spoke at great length to a crowd of his workers at Briton Ferry to urge them to enlist, telling them:

> A thousand times would I sooner see my sons die a glorious death on the battlefield than remain cowards at home...

On 2nd October news reached Carmarthen that the Welsh Field Company, Royal Engineers had recently moved from Pembrokeshire to Northampton. 95% of this group had volunteered for overseas service. As a result of their departure, recruitment for a reserve company began in the county and the call for tradesmen went out, the new unit being called the 2nd Welsh Field Company, part of the Territorial Force. Three men from Laugharne are known to have served with this unit: Charles Thomas Rowlands, of Gosport Street, John Evans Williams of The Corporation Arms, and Horace Sharman, of Port Lewis, Stoneyway.

Recruitment continued to be a major topic on the home front. *The Welshman* of 16th October printed an extract of a speech by Lord Henry Philipps of Picton Castle at a recruiting meeting at St Clears, presided over by Sir James Hills-Johnes, VC. The newspaper article said:

> As true Welshmen they must all realise the great crisis which had over-taken us as a nation and he felt that as gallant Welshmen they would not be behind, but would, as in the past, still maintain the noble traditions gained by them in their great days gone by. He asked the older people to encourage the young ones to come forward and to respond to their country's call and join the new Welsh Army Corps... Without in any way prejudicing the new Welsh Army Corps, he asked why Wales should not also have its own Welsh Guards Regiment.

So, in October 1914 the campaign began to lobby the War Office to create another regiment, the Welsh Guards, to serve alongside the existing Scots and the recently formed Irish Guards. Campaigners in West Wales, such as Lord Philipps, worked hard to lobby for their cause, resulting in the formation of the Welsh Guards by a Royal Warrant of 26th February, 1915. This new unit was to be another drain on the depleted resources of manpower from West Wales. Among their numbers were at least four men from Laugharne: Ivor Victor Wentworth George of Sea View, Cornelius Mortimer David of Pentrehowell, William Whitehead, and William Davies. Whitehead had been a servant at Milton Bank prior to enlisting and would be mortally wounded in France later in the war, dying at No. 25 Stationary Hospital, Rouen on 13th April, 1917.

On 7th December, 1914, the *Cambria Daily Leader* reported on another major aid to recruitment in Laugharne: Lance Corporal Fuller, VC, who visited his home town:

> VC'S VISIT TO LAUGHARNE. Lance-Corporal William Fuller, V.C. visited his native town, Laugharne, on Saturday night, and received a rousing reception. The motor-car in which he was being conveyed was "held up", and ropes being attached, the hero was drawn triumphantly through the streets, the procession being headed by torchlight bearers and Scout bugles. A halt was made at the Mariners' Corner, when Corporal Fuller thanked the inhabitants for the reception he had received, and hoped he would not be the only Laugharne boy to receive the coveted honour.

The visit was part of an organised recruitment campaign, the first of many in which this local hero would participate, which took him all around West Wales over the coming weeks.

Lists of new recruits filled the columns of the local newspapers, adding to the pressure upon others to follow, although there was a mere trickle of volunteers from Laugharne, who did not even merit a mention. For example, in the Amman Valley the local colliery saw 40 men leave to enlist into the army. The picture was similar in many other collieries and in major firms, such as the Lime Firms Company of Llandybie, and, throughout the county, farm workers, farmers' sons and labourers flocked to the colours. Many of these men were skilled workers who would prove hard to replace.

The Welshman had an interesting article within its pages on Friday, 18th December relating to the progress of recruiting for the second line units for the local battalions:

> Recruiting for the Reserve Battalion of the Pembroke Yeomanry at Carmarthen is going strong, with only sixty more men needed to complete its establishment of 469 Officers and men.... Good progress is being made in raising the Carmarthenshire Battalion of the Welsh Army Corps. Since August the numbers who have enlisted at Carmarthen for Kitchener's Army up to the end of last month was 567...

Meanwhile the Reserve Battalion of the 4th Welsh, stationed at the time at Carmarthen Barracks, had just received the honour of being inspected by Lieutenant-General Sir James Hills-Johnes VC. *The Welshman* reported:

> After brisk recruiting locally it was only a hundred men short of its full complement; of the number locally recruited, Llanelli had contributed 350, Llandeilo a hundred, Carmarthen seventy eight, Haverfordwest sixty four, Cardigan forty five and Pembroke twenty four.

At least seven men from Laugharne are known to have served with the 15th Welsh (Carmarthen Pals) during the course of the war. Some of these were very early enlistees into the battalion, who would embark for France on 2nd December, 1915: David Brown of The Lacques, Arthur Percy Davies of Morfa Bach, Richard James Davies of The New Inn, Pendine (whose parents were from Laugharne), 2nd Lieutenant Clifton Malet Lucas (whose great grandfather was from Laugharne), Frank Arthur Roberts of Hugdon, James Jeremy Roberts of Fernhill Cottage, and William David Thomas, born in Laugharne in 1898 but living with his parents in Treorchy.

Local recruiting was starting to fall – a national trend. Local newspapers began printing articles urging more men to volunteer and local dignitaries began arranging recruitment meetings around the county, many attended by regular soldiers who were home after being wounded in France and who spoke about their experiences during the fighting. The positive feelings which had spread over Britain at the outbreak of war were now disappearing as more and more casualties occurred.

At the end of 1914 recruitment figures for Carmarthenshire were released which, for a small county, were quite impressive. By then almost 3,700 recruits from the county had enlisted for the regular army.

It is impossible to know for certain how many men and women from Laugharne had enlisted during these early months of the war, but it was certainly quite a small number, as the majority of the troops in action were regulars. So in the main only regular soldiers and reservists had been in action. By the end of 1914 three men from Laugharne had been killed, and Captain Price Vaughan Lewes had died of natural causes.

In the New Year numbers of enlistees at Carmarthen during the first week of January proved disappointing, with the *Carmarthen Journal* reporting that 37 men had joined the 15th Welsh during that week.

As part of another recruitment exercise and to gain further publicity for the Battalion, a series of rugby matches was arranged throughout the county, whilst at the headquarters of the South Wales Mounted Brigade at Carmarthen recruits continued to pour in.

The *'War Jottings'* column in *The Welshman* of 28th May noted that 10 recruits from Llandyssul had been brought to Carmarthen by the recruiting lorry. It also reported that the Bishop of St David's, whilst making a speech at Tenby, had condemned the people of West Wales as being:

> ...very slow to take home to their hearts and minds the magnitude of the War and that they had not yet realised that we were fighting for our country.

This suggests that there was still some apathy in West Wales about the war, with many people thinking that the 'European' war was nothing to do with them.

There were, however, some emotional responses. For example, Thomas James Jackson, the young son of David and Harriet Jackson, was killed on 10th June, 1915, while taking part in an attempt to dislodge the Turks from a trench east of the Gully Ravine, Gallipoli. The death of his son caused David Jackson to attempt to re-enlist into the army. He had served for several years before getting married and moving to Laugharne, but was turned away for being over-age. The *Carmarthen Journal* of 23rd July, 1915 recorded his next move to gain revenge for his son:

> A dramatic incident occurred at a recruiting meeting at Laugharne on Tuesday. Impressive speeches had been delivered on the urgent necessity for more men, and a call was made for volunteers. The first to come forward was Mr D. Jackson, Holloway Road, Laugharne, who created a deep impression when he remarked, *Take me, please, I want to go out to avenge the death of my eldest son at the Dardanelles*. He was loudly cheered by the large crowd for his courage in offering his services. It may be recalled that the son referred to was reported killed at the Dardanelles last week. Commander Brayshay, RN, presided, and the chief speakers were Major Glossop, Captain Margrove, Sergeant Langdon, DCM, Captain Lloyd, Captain Cuffe, and Sergeant W. Fuller, VC.

Throughout 1915, recruiting parties continued trawling West Wales for men. On Sunday 10th October, a large crowd gathered at Tremoilet School, presided over by Morgan Jones, of Llanmiloe. The Reverend Phillips, of Pendine and Llandawke, was proud to be given the opportunity to speak at the meeting and was followed by Captain Margrave who pressed the need for men to the assembled crowd. There was no mention of any volunteers resulting from the meeting, although two men from Pendine: William Morgan, of Avola Stores; and George John, of Shore House, had enlisted the previous week.

The 15th Welsh Recruiting Car, photographed outside County Hall in Carmarthen. The car, driven by local officers, carried out a well-documented recruitment drive in the industrial towns of Farnworth and Bolton before seeking recruits in Carmarthenshire.

The 38th (Welsh) Division Rugby team, which ranked among the top divisional teams in the army.

Recruitment was probably hindered by the continuing bad news regarding local casualties. A report about the latest memorial service to be held at St Martin's Church to commemorate Laugharne's fallen soldiers on 24th October, was followed by several paragraphs reporting that numerous local men had been hospitalised due to wounds. Bad news from nearby St Clears was also reaching Laugharne, including the death in action of a postman, Corporal William Henry Owens of the 14th Hussars, and that Private Sydney Williams of the 4th Welsh, had been reported missing. Coupled with lengthy casualty lists from France and news that General Townshend's force in Mesopotamia was being forced to retreat to the city of Kut, none of this would have instilled much enthusiasm into young men to enlist.

The struggle to recruit men was a continuing concern at Government level, so a working party had been set up in order to look at how to improve the situation without resorting to forced conscription. 'The Derby Scheme' was proposed by Lord Derby as an attempt to increase recruitment by allowing men to voluntarily attest for service at a later date. Men who attested under the scheme would be paid a single day's wages, placed in the Class B Army Reserve and released to civilian life until needed by the military.

The scheme was originally intended to run only from 16th October to 30th November, 1915, but the number of men trying to attest under the Derby Scheme forced the authorities to extend it further until 15th December, 1915. Many recruitment offices were so overwhelmed that medical examinations were not carried out, as the men would be examined in the future when called up for service. Men who registered their name would be called upon for service only when necessary and married men were promised that they would only be called up when single men became unavailable. Men were classified in groups according to their year of birth and marital status and were to be called up with their group when it was required.

One of the Lord Derby Scheme armbands, worn by men who had already attested to serve in the Army but were yet to be called up.
(© IWM (INS 7764)

To enable people to identify those men who had attested to serve at a later date, a khaki armband was issued for wear. A man who had attested was also free to enlist fully at any time if he wished to. Benjamin Tucker was one such. He applied for the Forces but failed the medical test, so he reapplied several times, each without success. But Benjamin worked hard to do what he could. He managed to persuade Laugharne Corporation, against the wishes of some of its senior members, to be more flexible and allow servicemen to be sworn-in as Burgesses at the earliest opportunity, rather than at the immediate next Big Court after their coming of age (when they may be away on active service). This allowed them to retain the seniority they would have had and stay in sequence for obtaining the income – more significant then than now – from a share as they became available in the future.

Meetings were held all around the country to set up local committees to assist with the Derby Scheme. The *Carmarthen Journal* of 5th November, 1915 reported one such meeting at Laugharne:

> A recruiting meeting was held in the Town Hall on Monday afternoon, in support of Lord Derby's scheme. Mr Morgan Jones, Llanmiloe, was in the chair, supported by the Vicar of Laugharne (Rev. J. Thomas), Rev. G.P. Williams (curate), Rev. J.R. Phillips (Baptist), Mr Grant Dalton, and several others. The meeting pledged themselves to do everything in their power to further the scheme. Canvassers appointed for town and district are: Messrs. T. Brayshay, S. David, S.G. Dalton, John Jones, E.A. David, Evan Benjamin, T. Sharp (Plashett).

In the long run, the scheme proved less successful than hoped in that it did not result in the large numbers of enlistees required at the time, so it was abandoned in December 1915, to make way for the Military Service Act 1916, which introduced conscription.

Also in various local newspapers was a public request by the Government for more doctors for the Front, with a request that one in three doctors aged under 40 should enlist into the army. There were already several local doctors in France, including Captains Rowland Philip Lewis and Thomas Harold Thomas, of Laugharne.

These instructions referred to an immediate recruiting canvass of men eligible for military service who had not been exempted due to their occupations. The text of the instruction read:

> As it is evidently the duty of every man who has not been starred to at once join the Army, he being no longer required for necessary services in his country, you are to take whatever steps you consider most effective to induce such men to join the Army. In carrying out this you will doubtless be assisted by the local authorities.
>
> You should see in your district that no un-starred man is able to complain any longer that he is not wanted in the Army as he has not been fetched.
>
> You should report the number of non-starred men in your district who refuse to give their services to the country by enlisting in the Army, where they are so much needed.

Such was society's pressure on men to recruit that even those who were discharged after being wounded often needed some evidence to show that they were now exempted from service. The Silver War Badge was designed and implemented especially as a recognition of their service and it helped men whose outward appearance may not have shown they were discharged from service as a result of injuries.

On 30th November a farmers' meeting was held in the Gwalia Hall at St Clears in an attempt to bolster recruiting in the area. It was chaired by Captain Cremlyn, the local Recruiting Officer, who spoke at length. He then travelled to Laugharne and made a similar speech to crowds who had assembled around the Town Hall. The *Carmarthen Journal* had recently reported:

> Important as Agriculture is, especially in times like the present, farmers, together with other sections of the Community, have to make sacrifices. They must do with the least possible number of hands...

The Silver Wound Badge – Richard Pearce (right) with his uncle, Oliver Evans, and one of his brothers, Tommy, who is wearing the badge.

Cremlyn went on to mention the huge profits farmers were then making on cattle, due to shortage of supply and increased prices, and said that this profit should be re-invested into the war effort, not spent on pleasure. The *Journal* says he spoke at length over the character of the Germans and their sacrifices for the cause before asking the people at Laugharne:

> Were they equally patriotic? Had Welshmen done all they could for their country in this struggle? Had the people of Carmarthenshire made every possible sacrifice? Was every man in Laugharne physically fit, in the Army, or had he enlisted, or was he making ammunitions. Was everyone doing his bit to put Germany down and keep Britain up?

As a consequence, each applicant had to say how many of their family worked on the farm.

In February 1916 the first meeting of the Carmarthen Rural Tribunal heard appeals by individual men, or their employers, to be exempted from military service. The majority of cases were for farm workers or those whose job related to the land. Few were granted absolute exemption; for most the inevitable was merely postponed. One 62 year old Laugharne farmer, farming 140 acres with cattle, horses, sheep and pigs, appealed for two of his three sons. Temporary exemption was granted for one of the sons, the other was refused.

Many of the cases of local men were reported in the *Carmarthen Journal* and *Carmarthen Weekly Reporter*. They revealed a significant number of rabbit catchers in the Laugharne area. At least eight individual rabbit catchers appealed, though given the number of farms in the district, it is perhaps not surprising so many rabbit catchers would be needed. For example, at the end of July 1916 a record number of rabbits was caught locally by Mr Jim Edmonds, one of the six sons of Elizabeth Edmunds. The family had farmed Halldown Farm until the death of James' father David, when they moved to a smaller property at Llansadurnen. In eight nights he caught 900 rabbits, demonstrating the great need for local rabbit catchers. Most of the rabbits caught would have been sent to market out of the area, but no doubt a good number of them found their way on to the tables of families in Laugharne. In April Jim encountered the Appeals Committee:

> A Laugharne rabbit-catcher, who appealed, said he was a discharged soldier. On Jan. 13th, 1915, he enlisted voluntarily, and joined the 1st Life Guards. He was then given seven days' leave to dispose of his business, which he did at a great sacrifice, losing in the transaction at least £40. He returned to Carmarthen on the 7th, and was sent to London where he was in barracks until February 19th, when he was discharged as unfit. He had now re-purchased a stock of traps and snares, etc., and he had taken a number of farms on which to catch rabbits. To dispose of the business now would mean a great financial loss. Seeing that he had offered his services once and had been rejected, he thought it was hard to be called up again. Appellant produced his discharge, signed by Ld Penrhyn, which stated that he was unfit for duty in the Household Cavalry. Capt. Margrave: *He is not unfit for his Majesty's forces. He is only unfit for the Household Cavalry.* In view of his discharge certificate, appellant had not attested under the Derby Scheme, and he was directed to appeal again under the Military Service Act.

The same tribunal also heard the case of another rabbit catcher from Laugharne:

> A rabbit trapper in Group 6 appealed for exemption. He lived in the Laugharne district. Two brothers were in the Army and one in the Navy. He appealed on the ground of hardship. The Clerk (Mr J. Saer): *How many rabbits do you trap every year.* Appellant: *I only commenced to trap this winter. How many have you trapped? I can't say exactly. Can't you tell us to within a few hundreds? How many do you trap a week? About 40.*

Appellant said that he also set gardens. Capt. Margrave: *I think this man ought to go and the rabbits should have a chance like everybody else.* Appellant said that there was nobody to look after his mother. Capt. Margrave: *Your mother will come to no harm. We haven't the Germans over here yet.* Appellant said that he wanted time to set the gardens. He did not claim exemption altogether. Capt. Margrave said that it was pretty late to be setting gardens now. *The appellant would look much better in uniform than he looked now.* The Tribunal refused the application.

John James, a single man aged 37, farmed 43 acres of Corporation land at Upper Moor on a 21 year lease and had recently paid £200 to build a new house there. His appeal was refused and he joined the Navy, becoming stoker, 1st Class, fortunately surviving the war. A lady, eking out a living by selling eggs and butter from her smallholding of 4 acres, appealed on behalf of her son and was told the holding was 'so small that it did not count' and the appeal was dismissed.

While the first of the groups of county men to have enlisted under the Derby Scheme were leaving Carmarthen to join their units, a landmark moment in British military history occurred early in March 1916 when the Military Service Act was introduced by Prime Minister Herbert Asquith. The Act specified that men from 18 to 41 years old were liable to be called up for service in the army unless they were married, widowed with children, serving in the Royal Navy (there was no Royal Air Force until April 1918), a minister of religion, or working in one of a number of reserved occupations. A second act in May 1916 extended liability for military service to married men and a third act, in 1918, extended the upper age limit to 51. Men or employers who objected to an individual's call-up could, as earlier in the war, apply to a local Military Service Tribunal, which could grant exemption from service, but usually conditional or temporary.

Two more men from Laugharne were among the appellants at a tribunal at the end of May:

A hay merchant and farmer from Laugharne appealed for exemption for a married man who had five children. The Tribunal adjourned the case until the 1st July to enable the man to get a job in a munition factory and so release a single man for the Army.

A man who appealed stated that he was employed by Mr Morgan Jones, Llanmiloe. He said that he worked in the winter catching rabbits off the warren, and during the spring and summer on farm work. Capt.

Margrave: *There are lots of rabbit catchers down Laugharne.* Mr J.J. Bowen: *There are lots of rabbits there.* Capt. Margrave: *And a terrible lot of catchers too. We can do without a few of these catchers. Mr Morgan Jones has not appealed for this man, so probably he does not want him. We might turn him into a catcher of Germans and not of rabbits.* The application was refused.

Other local cases in the tribunal during July were of: James Roberts, the Laugharne ferryman; and John Pearce, a fish hawker, of Frog Street. The former appeal was dismissed, while John Pearce was granted a six week stay before having to re-appeal. During the following week's tribunal two more Laugharne men appealed: Mr Howells, of Parc Cynog, appealed against the conscription of Lewis Phillips, of Brook, who worked on his farm. His appeal was upheld, while an appeal by Ben Taylor, of Clifton Street, was adjourned until the following week.

An appeal for Merlin Rees Watts, aged 20, of Sarland Farm, Llansadurnen, was granted temporarily in November, 1916, until a replacement for him on the farm could be found by the military. Presumably one was found for him because he joined the Monmouth Regiment, suffered serious illness in March, 1917 and was awarded the Military Medal in November 1918.

A group photo of Welsh Regiment recruits at Press Heath,
showing a variety of ages from very young men to men in their fifties.

Henry Raymond, who farmed Honeycorse Farm and also managed Coygen Quarry, pointed out that not all necessarily went smoothly with the military replacements that were found for farmwork. He said that in 1917 he had three:

> One was a good man, but I could only have him for one week. The other two I could keep as long as I liked, but they were no good. I told one of them not to let the calves drink too much milk from the factory and he let two of them drink until they burst and died.

He had made an appeal on behalf of his traction engine drivers, Theophilus Howells and William Howell. The decision was postponed at that hearing but presumably was eventually refused as both entered the Army.

Back home two more men from Laugharne were appealing against their conscription notices:

> The *Carmarthen Weekly Reporter* of 21st June, 1918 noted:
> Joseph Williams, Brynonen, Laugharne, a road labourer, Grade II, aged 42, said that he was married and had seven children. He is in charge of an important length of road. He earned 28s a week. Lieut. Yorwerth: *We'll pay you better in the Army, although these gentlemen are your bosses. I'll give you a job making roads at better pay. Are you willing to go in for a better job?* Appellant: *I would rather not.* Mr E. Morgan, Surveyor, gave evidence in support of the appeal. *The war depts lorries used the roads in his district very much. This man and others were ready to assist the farmers when required.* Lieut. Yorwerth: *This man is a most important official of the Council, and he gets 28s a week.* Mr E. Morgan *I agree it is not enough.* Exemption until 1st November was granted.

The *Carmarthen Journal* of 28th June, 1918 reported that an appeal by William John, of the Carpenters' Arms, Broadway, Laugharne, had been declined and he was to enlist as required.

As a final note, the man who probably did most for the local recruitment effort during the war was Sir James Hills-Johnes, VC. The elderly gentleman survived the demands of the war, which had seen him attend more meetings and ceremonies than anyone else in the county, but he passed away at Dolaucothi on 3rd January, 1919, aged 85, a victim of influenza. An impressive funeral took place at Caio Churchyard, where Britain's oldest VC winner and a great man, was buried. Just the previous week he had unveiled one of the earliest village war memorials, at Manordeilo.

As a result of recruitment into the services, the shortage of labour for many activities at home – for mining, agriculture and teaching in particular – coupled with the pressure of rising prices, had the effect of empowering workers to join unions and press for higher wages. This was an unanticipated outcome of the Great War's recruitment campaign that was to last.

Chapter 2

Local Life in and around Laugharne

WAR IS DECLARED

When war was declared in August 1914, all over the country the gathering in of the harvest was well under way. Wheat, barley and oats all yielded well, the potato crop was believed to be so good that imports would not be needed for a whole year and prospects for the remainder of the harvest were reported to be good. As has been seen, the mood was generally one of optimism – the war was not expected to last more than a few months and, after an initial period of panic buying in the first few weeks, there seemed little concern about food supplies at this point.

It is not easy to discover how people felt in those early days of the war, especially from this distance in time; memories fade and usually did not get recorded. But it's possible to glean from tiny snippets that give clues to people's feelings. Fortunately one nearby source is available.

John James was a carpenter and wheelwright, based at Red Roses in the early decades of the 20th century. He worked for local farms such as Tremoilet and Brook. What is remarkable is that he kept a daily diary for which the years 1906-1909 and 1913-1915 are available. For this project his writings were researched for whether they reveal anything of the daily impact of the war on local lives.

He typically recorded what he did, whom he met and some family matters. So it is significant that suddenly on August 5th, 1914 he added the only piece of general news in more than three years of entries 'War declared between England and Germany'. Clearly for him it was an event of tremendous impact. In fact at the Declaration of War there were street celebrations in many parts

John James at his workshop in Red Roses.

of the UK! At the outset of the war it was widely anticipated that it would be 'all over by Christmas' and people were keen to relieve the tensions of the years building up to it and to get it over with – as they thought.

His entries continued:

> August 25: The Soldiers had entered Namur, that was the news today.

The Carmarthen Journal's Laugharne Notes recorded in mid August:

> The general topic of conversation is of course the war. The Post Office is beseiged on the arrival of the Postman by an eager crowd anxiously awaiting the morning papers to glean the latest news. Laugharne is well represented in the Army, Navy and auxiliary forces and we are proud of them.

But steadily the reality became clearer as the news of German progress mounted. James' diary continues:

> September 23: In the paper today 3 British ships sunk by Germans.
> October 12: In today's paper that Germans had taken Antwerp.

By October doubts were deepening and the next entries give indications of the fear and anxieties induced even here – so far from the war front:

October 14: The Thanksgiving Service was tonight at Roses Chapel. Thomas was preaching – he told me there was a German Spie passed this way about yesterday.

The spy story was the local gossip of the time – a party of young men had been seen descending on Laugharne from the direction of Llanstephan armed with notebooks in which they stopped every so often to note aspects of the landscape. All very mysterious – that is until it was revealed – some time later – that they were geology students from Swansea University out doing some field work in this area!

However, as a result of the discovery of a real German spy in the country, the Government rapidly introduced the requirement for a photograph in every passport – one of a number of requirements that were introduced for the war but which continue to this day.

Fears now grew, too, of a possible actual German invasion and James' next month's diary entries recorded:

November 16: The News came tonight that the Germans had landed in Yarmouth.

November 17: It was a false report by today that the Germans had landed.

Later that same month 'bombs' were discovered on the shore at Barks Point. Again that was a false alarm but is indicative of the underlying anxiety felt by local people.

In December news arrived that Scarborough, Whitby and Hartlepool had been shelled directly by the German Navy, killing 119, including children. It caused great shock all over the country. Just five days later Dover was bombed by aeroplane. The war front was no longer at a great distance; it was rapidly advancing here and casualties now included civilians. This was further confirmed in January by a Zeppelin bomb attack on East Anglia, the first of 51 such attacks.

Back in November, Laugharne had learned that a local man – William Charles Fuller – was to be awarded the first Victoria Cross to a soldier from Wales. For Mr Tyler (the local Headteacher) it was literally a red letter day as he changed his ink to a celebratory red to record the important news in the school log book. Imagine his excitement then when, later on, Fuller actually visited the Laugharne School!

School log book entry.

School Log Book entry 7 December 1914 – *the VC hero above referred to visited the school this morning and spoke very kind and encouraging words especially to the elder boys. The Lance Corporal received a very hearty acceptance – lusty cheers being given as he left. He promised us his photograph after he had received the coveted decoration. Lance Corporal Alex Newton of the 13th Glosters also visited us today.*

In these early months much of the local effort went towards supporting Belgian refugees, and Laugharne's support was so strong that a separate section of this book has been devoted to it.

As has been seen, from the outset of the war there was a daily drive to recruit men to fight. Posters even exhorted women to put pressure on their husbands and sons to join up. This left local women with tight incomes plus reduced support, whilst also under pressure to contribute or raise their children single-handedly! The Government gave some financial support – in 1914 it amounted to 12s 6d per week for the wife of a soldier or sailor and 2s 6d for each child – but it did not go far. At the same time everyone was being exhorted to raise cash, make articles of clothing and provide food for the war effort. Life must have been really hard for families here at home.

Within the first few weeks of the war the public were being encouraged to eat fish as a substitute for meat and other foods, as this would not have any effect on the national stock of food supplies. People were also encouraged to keep their own poultry and pigs. The chief categories of food needed were wheat, oats, potatoes, meat, milk and butter. At the outset of the war, Britain only produced about a fifth of the wheat it required, relying heavily on imports.

Imports of all foods and cheaper goods from the colonies were eventually to become badly affected by the German U-boat campaign, which sank thousands of tons of merchant shipping, and the Government began to try to raise home food production.

The Carmarthen Journal of 18th September, whilst noting the need for recruits and mentioning the passion being felt in the colonies to aid the mother country, also brought up the importance of the farmer in this great time of crisis. A national call went out for farmers to increase production of cereals; emphasising a need to ensure the best use of arable land to bolster the five months' worth of wheat and grain then remaining in Britain. There was a call to people to utilise their gardens fully for growing vegetables such as turnips and cabbages, and also to farmers to increase their cheese production. It was commonplace at the time for farmers to produce only enough cheese to serve their own needs but the Government, realising the importance of this high protein and long-keeping food, pressed farmers to step up production for sale. The beginning of industrial dairy production in Carmarthenshire can be traced back to this simple request in September 1914 – another long-lasting outcome of the war effort.

Laugharne was fortunate in having a good sprinkling of better-off families in comfortable homes where incomes were such that the women did not need to seek work and servants released them from domestic chores. So they had resources, and especially time, to help out with the war effort. They were not forced to do so but many of them rose to the occasion splendidly. Their numbers included Mrs Bolton, Mrs Peel, Miss Falkener, Dulcie Peel, Mrs Brayshay and Miss Cunningham.

Within a month of the outbreak of war the *Journal* had reported Ritso Bolton gazetted to the Royal Field Artillery and Stuart, his younger brother, off to the west of Ireland on HMS Doris. Their mother, Mrs Bolton, plunged herself into the war effort, as the local paper reported:

> …sparing nothing to be of service at this critical period. Her car has been at liberty for any useful purpose. She has also procured several sacks and straw which she has forwarded to the troops stationed in West Pembrokeshire.

Around Carmarthenshire meetings were held by the British Red Cross Society, to bolster interest in the institution and to gather funding and volunteers for service to help the allied soldiers and people of Europe who were suffering due to the war. It was also looking to supplement the work of the Royal Army Medical

Corps, which was soon struggling under the sheer volume of wounded. The Red Cross would also play a role in helping to trace the whereabouts, or the fate, of the many missing men.

At a meeting in Carmarthen in October the Carmarthen Board of Conservators held an enquiry about the low levels of fish stocks in the locality, with numbers of trout and salmon falling in the River Towy. Numbers of sea fish being caught were also dropping dramatically. Some local water bailiffs had been publically accused of failing in their duties and a hearing began in the middle of October to investigate the claims. Poaching was rife in the county and trawlers were operating illegally within the three mile limit. Cocklers were ruining the cockle beds at Laugharne and Ferryside by driving carts over the sands, resulting in dead cockles polluting the water.

The meeting agreed that the salmon fishing season would be shortened and that a summons was taken out against the trawler men. It was acknowledged, however, that nothing could be done to prevent the cockle gatherers from driving their carts on the beaches as there was no other way of bringing the heavy sacks of cockles ashore. Cockling was an important trade for Laugharne at that time.

William Griffith (left) outside the Ship & Castle in King Street.

In Laugharne, William Griffith opened a 'social club' in the Ship & Castle Inn, comprising a reading room, stocked with newspapers, and a billiard room which became well-used by local people. However, it confused some visitors who entered and seated themselves to await non-existent refreshments! Refreshments were, of course, available across the road in the Brown's Hotel, which William had also acquired on his marriage to Mrs Wilkins. There they placed the ballroom at the disposal of ladies who knitted garments for the war effort and, by the end of November, 104 bundles had been received in the Whitland District, to which Laugharne's knitters had contributed.

In November, too, Laugharne Gun Club was formally wound up and its funds, together with a collection, were donated to the Princess Mary Fund. King George's 17 year-old daughter, Princess Mary, proposed to send every person wearing the King's uniform a specially commissioned Christmas gift tin, typically containing an ounce of tobacco, a packet of cigarettes in a yellow monogrammed wrapper, a cigarette lighter, and a Christmas card plus a photograph of Princess Mary.

A smaller article noted the return home of Lance Corporal William Fuller, VC, of Laugharne, who had been shot in the arm at Gheluvelt. Fuller would never return to France, remaining in West Wales to campaign for recruits.

A Princess Mary tin.

A New Year 'Social', organised by Mrs Peel raised substantial funds to purchase wool for knitting garments for soldiers and sailors. It was to become a traditional event each year. By April she was able to forward 15 pairs of socks, 13 body belts, 14 scarves and 2 pairs of mittens. The ladies had been busy, and she treated them to a function held at the infants' school, with games, dances and refreshments to reward their efforts.

Farmers around the county began a series of meetings during March to debate the possibility of forming co-operatives for selling milk, cheese and butter. A resolution was passed to form the South-West Wales Dairy Farmers' Association, which would be able to better control the dairy market and ensure that a fair price was paid for local produce. One dairy had been built at Broadway, Laugharne, prior to the war, but mention was also made of the possibility of building another milk factory in the county along the same lines as the one already operating at Llandeilo. Other dairies would eventually be built at St Clears, Whitland, Carmarthen and Newcastle Emlyn. Farmers were encouraged to be more productive despite fewer employees, so Mr J.D. Morse took a lead, demonstrating the shearing of a large flock of Masham sheep at Dicky Lake using the latest type of shearing machine.

The local branch of the British Red Cross was still keeping itself busy. Notable members in the county included Lady Cawdor, who allowed her substantial home at Golden Grove to be used as a convalescent home for wounded men. Lady Lloyd took in wounded soldiers at her residence at Bronwydd and Mrs Lloyd did the same at Glangwili. Other local manors at Llwynbrian and Glanrhydw were also put to similar use. The men who were put up in the luxury of these grand houses had been discharged from local war hospitals at Llandovery and Carmarthen, with a dozen or so men arriving from a Cardiff hospital towards the end of March. Fundraising to help cover the costs of nursing these men was carried out by local Red Cross groups.

The war was about to take a considerable turn for the worse over the coming weeks, and these local war hospitals and Red Cross groups would soon be tested to the limit.

Families here became more and more anxious as worrying news came back of attacks and of losses on many war fronts. Letters home were important sources of solace. For example, Thomas James Jackson was slightly wounded shortly after the landings, and wrote home to his parents at Holloway Road, Laugharne:

I am alright now. When we landed we had a fine reception and we went for the Turks like mad dogs let loose and soon shifted them. We were not long about it either. We sent them over the hill and we held the position for a few days. We were relieved by the French and then we joined our brigade and had a great battle. Had they not shifted we would have wiped them out. It is a funny feeling when you charge with the bayonet. When you are halfway you don't aim for anything. We fought a good many fights before I was hit, but I am going to do my share again. Please send me some paper and envelopes.

Soldiers who were home on leave would be welcomed for themselves and also for their news. Throughout April a number of soldiers were home on leave in Laugharne, two of whom were the brothers Alfred and David Lewis, sons of John Lewis, of Hugdon. They were pre-war regulars enjoying their first leave at home together since joining the forces several years previously. Also home on leave was Thomas William Arnold Evans, 14th Welsh, of Market Street, who had been using his skills as a butcher by becoming the camp slaughterman at Rhyl; William Constable, of the 15th Royal Welsh Fusiliers (RWF); Richard McConnell, of the North Staffordshires; and Cyril Newton, of the Army Service Corps. News that John Parry, 2nd Welsh, had been wounded and hospitalised also reached Laugharne, but he was stable and had been recommended for the Distinguished Conduct Medal (DCM). At the same time dozens of families around the county were in mourning for their lost sons.

The Ladies Sewing Guilds continued to be busy sewing and knitting comforts to send out to the men at the front. An article in *The Carmarthen Journal* listed the garments:

> Forty three pairs of socks, twenty two body belts, fifteen helmets, seventy three mufflers, thirty eight pairs of cuffs, sixty pairs of mittens, twenty nine shirts, ten pants, one suit, and three coats.

Standing out among all the military news, a small paragraph in *The Welshman* of 10th September reported the not unsurprising news that local farmers were beginning to feel the shortage of manpower to labour on their farms and that work was under way to recruit more farm servants.

By now local children were also engaged with the war effort, sending boxes of flowers to the Red Cross Hospital to cheer up the wounded there and egg collections became a regular service encouraged by Mr Tyler through the National School.

The local hero, William Fuller, VC, was discharged from the army following his recovery and he toured West Wales, helping in the recruiting process. The story of him getting into a lion's cage during a fair at Fishguard to prove his courage circulated in the county, but some less flattering stories prompted Fuller to announce in *The Carmarthen Journal* that stories of him being intoxicated whilst on recruiting duties at the Cothi Bridge Show were untrue and that he had never tasted intoxicants in his life! He had recently been involved in a serious accident while on a recruitment drive in west Wales, when the chauffeur of the motor car in which he was travelling lost control and crashed outside Fishguard, throwing several occupants over the side of a bridge.

Loos was soon to claim the life of that popular Laugharne man, Lieutenant John Ritso Nelson Bolton, when he was killed on 27th September. By the end of May 1915, John had been mentioned in despatches for bravery. On 25th September, 1915, his gun battery was on active duty at Vermelles, taking part in the massed artillery bombardment on the German lines. John was acting as Forward Observation Officer that day when he was wounded and brought back to Foquières where he died two days later. He is buried in Foquières Churchyard Extension, Pas-de-Calais, France. He had been recommended for the Distinguished Service Order on the morning of his wounding but, sadly, because the award is not awarded posthumously, it was never sanctioned!

The 14th Battery, 22nd Brigade, Royal Field Artillery in France, 1914, proudly nursing their catch for the pot! Laugharne's John Ritso Nelson Bolton is the smiling front row young officer without a moustache.

Throughout September newspaper column space was filled with row upon row of names of the fallen, the wounded, and of gallant deeds in Flanders and at Gallipoli (from the previous month). Llanelli and Llandovery Hospitals were swamped with badly wounded men and Carmarthen Hospital received 22 wounded men, mostly ANZACs (Australia and New Zealand Army Corps).

Fears of further bombing of the mainland here led the Government, at the start of 1915 and under all-embracing powers given by the Defence of the Realm Act (DORA), to introduce restrictions on lighting at night. This was one of the earliest restrictions to be imposed on everyday life, though its full enforcement took another year to be imposed on Laugharne. Over the space of just a few months enthusiasm on the Home Front had waned, turning to fright for their own lives here in their homes and the realisation that the war could seriously impact upon daily lives here in Laugharne.

Henry Raymond of Honeycorse.

But Laugharne's gentlefolk still showed a commitment to the welfare of Laugharne people, especially if they fell on hard times. And, with time being available to them as well as comfortable finances they were able to lead local responses to the war. Thus *The Carmarthen Journal* reported that Miss Cunningham of Mapsland and Henry Raymond of Honeycorse were among the first to donate gifts of fruit and vegetables to the Mayor's War Relief Fund. Miss Falkener of Glanymor and Mrs Bolton of Elm House were both active in raising funds for the Soldiers and Sailors Families Association; Morgan Jones of Llanmilo frequently gave donations to the Prince of Wales Relief Fund and to the Lord Lieutenant's Fund, whilst Misses Morgan Jones, of Llanmilo, and Dulcie Peel, of Fernhill, gave donations to the Penny Fund for Sick and Wounded, and Mr Eccles of Broadway Mansion chaired the Hospital Management Committee in Carmarthen.

However, the (unnamed) less well-off people of Laugharne were also generous as a jumble sale held in September 1916 raised over £60 for the wounded. This was a huge sum at the time, in fact far exceeding those individual donations mentioned above.

By the autumn of 1915, it was apparent the war was not going to end soon and the Government was becoming concerned about the country's ability to provide itself with enough food. But there was no move yet to introduce a system of rationing for the whole country. Instead, Lord Selborne, the Minster for Agriculture, established War Agricultural Committees in each county. These were collaborative efforts between the Board of Agriculture and each County Council and they were tasked with increasing agricultural production and managing the limited resources in their own area. There were two committees for this county, one for the Borough of Carmarthen and one for the rural district of Carmarthenshire, and both met in the county town. Calls were growing for women to work on the land as more men and were being called up for the Front, and large numbers of horses had also been requisitioned for the Army. Farmers were also increasingly being criticised for higher prices although food shortages inevitably led to inflation.

In many areas of the UK boy scouts helped in the war effort – guarding bridges etc. We have no records that the Laugharne troop engaged in such activities, though it is difficult to imagine that Mr Tyler would have held them back from doing so. When war broke out he had helped to initiate the Refugee Committee and was invited to serve on it in June 1915.

Current local resident, Jeff Watts, remembers being told by his mother and his Aunty Lou about the daily news collection demanded by Mr Tyler (see panel). With each loss of life the flag inside the school was lowered to half-mast – a reminder for the children of the effects of war.

...something they dreaded doing... during the war. Every morning at break-time, the head-teacher, Mr Tyler, would choose two senior pupils to go to Laugharne Post Office. There they would obtain the latest news of World War I from the postmaster, Mr Ladd-Thomas. The news often included a list of local casualties. Sometimes there was a telegram which brought mainly bad news – a fatality. The senior pupils were often very upset, because they knew all the casualties personally. In fact, as they said, they were not much younger themselves than many of these casualties.

Almost every week the senior pupils brought back bad news from the Post Office. Either a soldier had been wounded, or sometimes killed.

He also encouraged his school pupils to take part in the war effort. From *The Welshman:*

24th September 1915: "The National School received thanks for the 200 eggs collected by the children. The letter thanked Miss Hubbard and Mr Tyler and the children of Laugharne schools for their very kind gift. Each child wrote their name on their egg.

Mr Tyler also kept a record, which was frequently published in the local press, of the numbers of ex-Laugharne school pupils engaged in the war, and submitted a report on them at the end of the war.

Indeed, so engaged was he in supporting the war effort that when this anonymous letter, below, was sent to *The Welshman* on 25th June, 1915, the local rumour was that it was he who had sent it. That led to his published denial on 2nd July, confirmed by the editor (below):

LETTERS TO THE EDITOR. LAUGHARNE SLACKERS – A WARNING. Laugharne compares favourably for recruits with any other town in the Principality. The little place has already paid a heavy toll... But a few of us notice that when the present stalwart "boys" return on furlough, a few slackers, not a dozen all told, jeer at them as they pass and waste on them their empty wit. These shirkers belong to the parasitic half-idling class; they are failures themselves, unclean breeders of their kind and immoral snipers who ruin the integrity of the young community. With a lopsided gait they parade the streets and defend the corners and lounging seats with their filthy tongues and cigarettes. Honour they have not, cowardice and indecency are the natural issues of their weak character... Had they the sense of duty they would have joined Kitchener's Army. A PATRIOT.

Followed by:

LETTERS TO THE EDITOR. LAUGHARNE SLACKERS – A DISCLAIMER. I never have been and sincerely trust I never shall be the author or instigator of an anonymous letter of any character whatsoever. Yours, R.H. Tyler. [The Editor confirms that the letter was written by a different man].

The pressure for everyone to engage in the war continued to increase. In August 1915 a Registration Act was passed, similar in manner to the census of 1911, and it took place on the night of Sunday 10th August. Everyone between the ages of 15 and 65 was registered and categorized according to their age and occupation. Men not already in the armed forces were allocated a "class" which would determine their suitability for military service, or whether they would remain in a particular occupation if it was in the national interest. Once analysis of the National Register was complete, men whose "class" was closely related to agricultural work would not be accepted for enlistment even if they offered themselves. However these exemptions were subject to change or sometimes even cancelled according to the needs of the War Office. The National Register revealed almost one and half million men who could be eligible to serve and so conscription was introduced for the first time. Lord Derby then introduced the scheme described in chapter one.

As a result of the shortage of agricultural workers and the loss of horses on farms, farmers were forced to change their practices and introduce mechanisation, and several local farmers led the way. In the Laugharne district, for example, in addition to the newest shearing machines being demonstrated by Mr J.D. Morse in 1915, Mr Gleed of Globe House purchased several Hampshire and Suffolk ram lambs at Northampton Ram Fair for local farmers and dealers to buy in order to introduce new stock to the area. One year later the lambs had produced excellent stock and there were plans to purchase more rams. Another enterprise by local butcher Mr Hubert Griffiths was the purchase of some Belgian hares in October 1915, from which he proposed to raise stock to sell for consumption. The hares were to be kept in hutches and fed corn and meal and would develop to a great size and weight in a short time. It is not recorded whether this was a success.

Gradually the shortage of men for work led to a recognition that women might be able to do the work – what a novel thought! It took some time to come about though, and then only gradually. The first – condescending – mention in the local papers came in September 1915 and related to the novelty of lady postal workers (see panel).

The Welshman: **24th September, 1915**
We are coming quite used to the lady "postmen", or as we should properly observe "postal carriers". Miss Sarah J. Wright has for some time taken the early delivery on one of the town routes. Owing to indisposition of Mr Bland, Miss Rena Williams is undertaking his duties. Both these young ladies show a thoroughly business-like manner in their new sphere of occupation.

29th October 1915: On Sunday a memorial service to local war heroes was conducted by the vicar (the Rev. J. Thomas, M.A., R.D.), the curate (the Rev. Gordon Williams, B.A.) and the Rector of Henllan (the Rev. W.L. Davies, M.A.). The following officers and men from Laugharne have fallen in the war:

Second-lieutenant Eric W. Wilson, West Yorkshire Regiment, killed in action in France;

Engineer-commander T.M. Davies of H.M.S. Hawke, lost in the North Sea;

Carpenter J.E. Thomas of H.M.S. Hawke, lost in the North Sea; Acting Leading Seaman R. Douglas Sealey, died of wounds at the Dardenelles;

Pte T. Jackson, South Wales Borderers, killed at the Dardenelles;

Second Lieutenant L.G.M. Smith, Royal Inniskilling Fusiliers, killed in France;

Lance Corporal K. Waters, Australian Forces, died of wounds at the Dardenelles;

Second Lieutenant J. Ritso Bolton, Royal Field Artillery, killed in France.

In that same month, on September 25th, 1915, Mrs Bolton received a telegram from the War Office stating that Ritso had been wounded in France, and within a week, another stating that he had died. Given his popularity such news impacted hard not only on the family but on the whole population of Laugharne. To make matters even more unbearable, eight months later came the report that his brother, Stuart, had also been lost in the sinking of HMS Indefatigable. Yet still Mrs Bolton continued to support the population in many ways – providing teas at sporting events, and using her premises for fund-raising functions.

Another Laugharne stalwart was Mrs Peel of Fernhill. Early in the war she had been busy collecting fruit and vegetables from the area, which she delivered personally to the 4th Welsh at Dale, with the assistance of Mrs Bolton and her motor car. She actively supported the refugees, serving on the organising committee as treasurer, making gifts of clothing, and warmly welcoming their arrival. In addition to the New Year 'social' she held a garden party later in the year to raise more funds and she served on the committee to raise money for the Soldiers and Sailors Fund. As time went on and evidence of poverty grew among the people of Laugharne itself she joined other philanthropists to raise cash and gifts for the poor of the Township. Tirelessly she continued to organise fund-raising events such as the Rose Day in aid of Carmarthen Infirmary. Not for nothing did she become known as the 'Angel of Laugharne'. She, too, was a single parent, her husband having died before the war; suffering the continual anxieties of having two sons actively engaged on active service. One of her sons, William Neville Hurt Peel, had enlisted in Canada into the 8th Battalion, CEF (Canadian Expeditionary Force). He was reported as *missing in action* on the 28th April, 1917, and she endured nearly a month of uncertainty before he was confirmed as killed in action.

Social events continued in Laugharne, with a visiting dramatic company performing each night over a week in November. But even their play, 'A Red Cross Nurse', had a military theme and the entire proceeds of one night were donated to the Red Cross.

By December Mr Tyler had arranged for a local garden close to the school to be used so that 'the older boys will be taught gardening and nature study'. Growing vegetables for home consumption was of course a highly emphasised element of the war effort. For Billy Lewis it proved the start of a career in gardening, and he became well-known locally as a brilliant gardener.

In November 1915 children in country districts were urged to help increase the home production of food. If their parents were keeping pigs or other livestock (and many in the Laugharne area would have done), in order to reduce the cost of feeding these animals, it was suggested they should collect

Laugharne School Gardening Club: Billy Lewis is fourth from the left.

Three Headteacherss – Mr Bradshaw (back),
Mr Tyler and Mr Miles Phillips.

William Consable.

acorns and horse chestnuts, rough grass etc. for use as fodder and to reduce the amount of straw used for litter, by collecting dried branches, grass and reeds.

By now the expectations of the nation for young men to join up proved too strong to resist and like many others, aged just 17, William Constable enlisted in Finsbury into the Royal Welsh Fusiliers, adopting a new uniform, as the photo shows. We follow more about him in chapter three.

1916

At the beginning of 1916 Lord Selborne had suggested that more women should be encouraged to work on the land. This was not an appeal to the wives and daughters of farmers who already worked on their own farms, feeding poultry, milking cows, helping with the harvest and so forth. This was a much wider appeal, especially to middle and upper-class women. He thought to take advantage of the deferential class structure of the time in that if the "ladies" of the district could be persuaded to volunteer then it would become "fashionable" for everyone else to take part.

Bakers often found it difficult to supply enough bread, so housewives were encouraged to bake their own. This would not, however, have been news to those in outlying rural communities who already baked their own loaves as they would not have been able to go to town frequently enough to buy fresh bread. A reduction in the price of flour in March 1916 was greeted with delight in Laugharne, but the question was whether it would affect the local price of a loaf. The pointed comment was made in *The Carmarthen Journal*:

> ...local bakers do not read the newspapers when there is a price reduction but immediately there is an increase, there is a rush to the newsagents.

By March 1916 women's labour was becoming more organised. District representatives were appointed for each area in the county with a Registrar for each village or group of villages, who would determine the available labour by starting with a public meeting followed by house-to-house canvassing. The Registrar would put farmers in touch with the women. At a public meeting in Carmarthen in April of the Women's Farm Labour Committee, several members addressed the meeting, including Miss Ethel Falkener, Registrar for the Laugharne District. Miss Falkener was just the kind of upper-class lady it was thought would galvanise support in her local district. A mature lady in her 40s and of independent means, she lived at Glanymor, a large mansion with extensive grounds overlooking the Taf estuary (now "Seasons" holiday park).

Fear of air raids led the police to advise the Corporation of Laugharne not to light street lights any more. So the street lamplighter was notified not to continue his daily rounds, and people out after dark had to feel their way home on dark nights.

The country reached a crisis point in April 1916 when it was estimated that only 6 weeks supply of wheat stock remained and coal stocks were rapidly running out. In Carmarthenshire it seemed the foods of most concern to the population were bread, butter, sugar and meat, as these featured most regularly in the columns of local newspapers. The War Agricultural Committee had arranged for boys over 12 who had passed the 5th standard and made the required number of attendances to be allowed out of school for the summer months to work on farms. It was advocated that girls could also work on farms, but by the end of January in Carmarthenshire only 8 boys and 4 girls in total had been excused. By contrast, the highest number excused was in Glamorgan with 46 boys and 3 girls.

By May the Board of Agriculture was asking for masters and boys of secondary schools to assist with the harvest, if the vacation could coincide as near as possible with the hay harvest. Schools would already be closed when the corn was harvested, and it would have been surprising if Mr Tyler had not been one of those responding to this call.

By now postal rounds might have been acceptable for women, but accepting women's ability to work on farms proved more of a challenge, despite the fact that many farmer's wives had done so over time immemorial. Consequently, in April there was an 'experiment' to see what women were capable of (see panel). Attitudes were slowly changing – but only under pressure of necessity.

> **The Welshman: 14th April, 1916**
> *LAUGHARNE NOTES & NEWS. The scarcity of labour is already being felt in the neighbourhood. In consequence of the enlistment at one local farm, only one ineligible man was left with a female servant. To prove the possibility of female labour in a case of emergency it was decided at this farm to try an experiment in manure spreading. The man carried the bags to the field, the maid sowed the manure and the employer kept them supplied with refreshment. The result was 2 tons of manure were sown by 6 o'clock.*

With May came an evening talk in the school room by Mrs Sylvia Roberts, the organising agent, to promote female labour. The meeting was 'well-attended' and by June *The Welshman* was able to report more instances of female employment (see panel).

> **The Welshman: 9th June, 1916**
> *Female labour is increasing daily in the district. A few have com-menced work in the Burry Port Munitions works and several others are contemplating starting in the next few days. A female haulier is continually with the District Council Scavenging Cart. Also a female letter carrier in Miss S. John who has taken the Bwlchnewydd route hitherto worked by Mr Austin Edwards who has gone to the munitions works.*

Miss Falkener, as Registrar for the Laugharne Women's Farm Labour Committee, took a lead here. On 3rd May Laugharne's women opened a garden on land belonging to Miss Falkener, to grow food produce for the neighbourhood. The garden was on the Cliff near to Glanymor and was described as having a southerly aspect, sheltered by high walls and containing some fruit trees, according to a report in *The Welshman*. Evidently it had not been cultivated for some time as it required a great deal of preparation. A garden plough was lent by Mr Hubert Griffiths, pulled along by the 'old white pony of Glanymor' and the ground was treated with a liberal dressing of manure. A good number of people turned up to help with the work, and donations in kind or to the 'tool fund' were gratefully accepted.

It was intended to utilise the walls for the cultivation of tomatoes in the coming season and to grow winter vegetables. Once set up, the garden was worked by 67 local women, who each had their own plot to cultivate. This became a big war garden and large quantities of vegetables were being grown by them. The Chairwoman of the Women's Farm Labour Committee held up Laugharne as an excellent example of what could be achieved. She claimed that women could do this work in their "spare" time and not have to walk a long way to reach where they intended to work, unlike working on farms. So successful was this garden at producing vegetables that Miss Falkener wrote to the Committee for instructions regarding sending vegetables to the fleet in response to a campaign appealing for fresh vegetables for "Jack Tars" which had begun in England soon after the outbreak of war. There came an urgent appeal for food by Lord Plymouth in September of 1916 and a group of ladies in Carmarthen resolved to set up a depot in the town for collecting the vegetables and sending them to the fleet. Whilst the drive and energy of our local leading ladies no doubt led to many benefits, sometimes it would seem they went a little too far, with Mrs Brayshay reportedly:

> ...supervising the children and homes of many absent soldiers, whose wives through ignorance, carelessness or bad habits, cannot be trusted to do their duty!

Nevertheless women land workers were also becoming increasingly frequent in the county, with young hay pitchers at Laugharne reported as acquitting themselves 'right well'.

As if the Government did not have enough on its hands, news of an Irish rebellion at Dublin also appeared in the newspapers during the month, telling of a declaration of a Republic and of fighting which had occurred there over Easter. Significant numbers of soldiers, better needed at the front, would be tied up with the Irish unrest for the remainder of the war.

Mrs Constable received a letter from William which shows how appreciated the gifts from home were, and also how experiencing life at the Front was changing this young man's outlook and ambitions:

April 10th 1916

My Dear Mother
I have just received your nice parcel, my word it was a good one. I like the nice little cook, also the sponge cake, the butter is handy as we don't get much of it, the cigs are allright. The bacon I soon got through. Mama that is just the parcel I like always something good you know. I had a parcel from Dada last week he sent me some socks and cigs. He told me Nev is getting on allright he said he is going to try and get him in some trade as an apprentice well Mama I won't go back into the drapery after I have finished with the army, to quiet a life for me, I should like to go on board ships, or go out to Canada farming, that would just suit me. We are having lovely weather out here just now. It has been like summer for this last month. We are getting as brown as berry by the sun.
From your soldier son, William.

May 1916 saw another historic moment in British history – the announcement of the decision to put into effect 'Daylight Saving Time'. The scheme was introduced for the duration of the war and started on the weekend of 20th – 21st May, when the clocks would be put forward one hour, and not put back until 1st October at 2 am. The main reasons were to reduce the hours of street lighting (thus saving on coal and gas) and to increase the number of daylight hours. Although envisaged as a temporary war measure it is, of course, still annual practice.

In Laugharne the war was proving to be a boon to the cockle industry. One merchant, John Howell Williams, a farmer and fish merchant from Laugharne, had moved to Portfield Gate, Haverfordwest, but received his supplies of cockles from his two sisters in Laugharne. He spoke quite openly to a reporter from the *Haverfordwest and Milford Telegraph*, telling them how much money he made from cockles, and that Laugharne was now exporting some three to four tons of the shellfish a week. A young girl from Laugharne, Mary Brown, cousin to Sergeant George Brown, worked for Mr Williams and lived at his home, Tonna House. It was there that she met and married a young man from Haverfordwest, James Richards, who would, however, soon be off to war – never to return.

Wartime regulations reached so many aspects of daily life that it could be difficult to keep up with them. Among other news during June was the story of a farmer at St Clears, William Rees Lewis, of Glasfryn Farm, who was charged with using the headlights on his motor car within six miles of the sea, contrary to the Defence of the Realm regulations. Lewis was fined 10 shillings, even though anyone knowing the area would realise that there was no possibility of the lights reaching the sea from Glasfryn!

A good number of men from the county were home on leave during June. Several of them were migrants from the county who had left before the war to build their future in the colonies; one such was Private James Price of the Canadian Highlanders. They also included a large number of sailors, fresh from their ordeal at Jutland, including Bridgeman Mordaunt-Smith, who told vivid tales of his experiences during the great battle. By now 150 men and boys had signed up to the colours, whilst those at home had contributed about £830 to charities directly connected to the war. In addition, over 200 horses had gone from the district for war purposes, with another score waiting to go.

The presence of female labour was now more common, though it still attracted comments and a degree of condescension. Miss Woodward had reopened Broadway cheese factory and soon Mary Pearce was appointed to take over from her father with the responsibility of operating the public weighbridge on the Grist.

In June local new potatoes were sold for 4½d per pound but by the following year the price had risen to 6d and then 8d per pound. There was a growing concern that 'the working man' could not afford the price of seed potatoes in order to grow their own. The vagaries of the weather also played a part in the success or otherwise of the crop. Potato rot was causing some concern locally in October 1916 due to the continuous rain. The following year, the County War Agricultural Committee encouraged the spraying of potatoes. An official from the Committee visited Laugharne and gave a demonstration at The Elms garden of Mrs Bolton. The Parish Council then arranged spraying for all those who wished to take advantage of the offer. It was believed spraying would increase healthy crops by 25%, prevent disease and produced healthier seed potatoes.

Meanwhile, the long lists of wounded made depressing reading, with papers such as *The Carmarthen Journal*, *The Welshman* and *The Western Mail* filling column upon column with names of casualties. The staggering number of casualties suffered by the Allies during the Somme offensive could be seen by reading *The Times Casualty Supplement,* which published the main casualty lists, listing them by regiment. By the time the Somme offensive would draw to an end, over 400 men from Carmarthenshire would be dead.

Probably a sign of the pressures on local people especially to feed their families, was that crime had again crept up in the county. At the Carmarthenshire Standing Joint Committee quarterly meeting on Wednesday 12th July, Chief Constable W. Picton-Philipps reported another surge in crime in the county since the last meeting – an increase of 335 crimes over the previous year.

This time drunkenness had decreased, but a surge in juvenile crime, chiefly theft, worried the committee. Cases of people failing to pay their rates had also increased disproportionately, with 208 out of the total of 1,419 crimes during the last three months due to that fact, most of them in Llanelli. Dudley Drummond of Hafodneddyn, Llangathen, one of the committee members, blamed the rise in juvenile crime on the cinemas, so a motion was passed to censor any films being shown.

Several families in Laugharne received letters at the end of August from sons who had arrived in France to replace the depleted battalions on the Somme. Among the men were: William Pearce, of Horsepool Road; Richard Edwards, of Morfa Bach; William Beynon, of Broadway; and David Edwards, of Llansadurnen. Richard Edwards was never to see his home town again. News also reached Laugharne of the severe wounds suffered by Austin Edwards, of Victoria Street, who had been seriously injured following an explosion at Llanelly Steel Works.

August found the Army Council pressured to release 27,000 soldiers to help with the harvest, including 900 for South Wales, but the following week these arrangements were cancelled, due to military necessity. In October, the Board of Agriculture declared no more farmworkers were to be called up until 1st January, 1917 in order to maintain production of food supplies, to allow autumn cultivation, and to review the agricultural situation. A few farmers, including Mr J. Evans of Hurst House and Mr H. Raymond of Honeycorse, purchased labour-saving milking machines to help them meet the demand for milk using less labour. In November Mr J.D. Morse purchased yearling pedigree Lincolnshire bulls, which were sold to improve the farming stock and a similar purchase was repeated the following year.

News of men on leave and other enlistees into the forces was also published: Frank Howell, of Causeway Farm, had volunteered to join a unit of the Machine Gun Corps in France; and George John, of Gosport Street, although still under age, had travelled to Cardiff to enlist into the Welsh Regiment. Bridgman Mordaunt-Smith was home on leave; as was William Howells, of Marros, who was recovering from wounds suffered in Salonika. News was also received by several Laugharne families from their sons in France.

Meanwhile the pressure on labour to work long hours at a higher productive rate, together with inflationary price rises was having an adverse effect on the workforce. So, although men were losing their lives on the Somme, it did not lessen militancy back home. A large rally at Cardiff voted in favour of a South Wales railway strike, to take effect on 17th September, unless their demands were met. A compromise was hurriedly agreed upon, averting the strike, awarding the railwaymen 10 shillings war bonus per week.

22nd September 1916: St Martin's Church, Laugharne was crowded on the occasion of a memorial service to six fallen heroes, whose names were read out:

Private W. Bevan;
Private David Bevan;
Private Daniel Davies;
Private Isaac Brace;
Lance Corporal Thomas Parry;
Midshipman Stuart Bolton.

The miners had also been pressing for more pay, looking for a 12½ percent increase in their wages to cover the higher cost of living. Their mood was not good after a tribunal turned down the request, especially when the Government began to press for more miners to enlist in the army. To add further insult, it was reported that three Ammanford miners were arrested in September for being absent from work and a riotous situation had to be resolved by one of their union men. Grumblings of discontent were still coming from the mining communities in the Amman and Gwendraeth Valleys and stinging criticism of their attitude was being hurled at them by disgruntled members of the public. Men serving in the armed forces also expressed anger at the miners, railwaymen and munition workers who were threatening strikes while the security of the Empire was at stake.

An outcry occurred at Llanelli after local newspapers printed details of the 2,000 Irishmen who had found work at the Pembrey explosives factory, thus becoming 'starred men', who would be exempt from military service. With the continuing push to call tinplate workers up for service, there was a lot of anger that these skilled local men would have to go to war while 'foreign labour' would be safely sat at home in Pembrey and Llanelli occupying jobs the locals should have been undertaking.

Some good news was received in Laugharne, however, by the parents of John Rochfort Williams, of King Street. The young soldier had so impressed his superiors during his first six months in France with the Royal Fusiliers that he was commissioned on 25th September as a Second Lieutenant into the 8th East Surrey Regiment.

Cinema-going was still really popular. By 1916 audience numbers nationally had reached 20 million per week, and the cinema superstar Charlie Chaplin was reported as receiving an annual salary of £127,000! A cinema had been established in Laugharne by 1914, renewed in 1915 under the management of A.W. Thomas and Hubert Griffith. Even here the war featured. In August 1916 the film *The Battle of the Somme* was shown – first in London – and within a week it had been viewed by more than 20 million people. Newspapers all noted the coming of the film with great interest and each showing was packed out. News was also coming into the county of some of the dozens of local men who had been awarded gallantry medals after their bravery during the Somme.

One notable event recorded in local newspapers in November 1916 was an announcement that the Government was placing Welsh collieries under the control of the Munitions of War Acts. This, effectively, nationalised them by placing the coal trade under the control of the Government in an attempt to allay fears of a strike after months of wrangling. During the month, the various unions of the county's dockers, smelters, gasworkers and tin and shotmen met at Llanelli to discuss the position of their industries.

In December 1916 there were public protests and meetings held at the Guildhall in Carmarthen against higher food prices. Locally there were letters in the local press complaining about the cost of food, often criticising farmers, and airing concerns about various shortages. Since food was controlled by each county council the response to higher prices and shortages varied from county to county. In Carmarthenshire it would appear the Council handled it quite well since the response was fairly restrained compared to other places like Devon where riots and angry mobs gathered and boycotts of local markets took place.

By the close of 1916 the year had cost the county of Carmarthenshire over 600 men dead and many more wounded. The total for the county was over 1,100 men dead since the outbreak of war. Laugharne had suffered the loss of 37 men linked to the Township, not all of whom are commemorated on the war memorial.

Several local soldiers and sailors came home on leave over the festive period. Among the men was Sergeant James Jeremy Roberts, of the 15th Welsh, who had been mentioned in despatches and promoted to sergeant as a result of his gallantry in the field. James had taken part in the severe fighting at Mametz Wood during the famous battle there from 7th to 12th July the previous year. News also reached Laugharne of the award of the Military Medal for bravery in the field to Able Seaman Arthur Reginald Morris, of the Royal Naval Division. His unit had seen severe fighting in the Ancre Valley of the Somme over the winter of 1916, and Reginald's award was well-deserved for the hell he had been through.

At home the Defence of the Realm Act, or DORA as it was called, governed all aspects of the war and, in December it reached a new peak. Under this act the 'Regulation of Meals' order came into force, restricting the eating of meat. Today this would seem a most extreme measure, as it applied to both public eating and in private houses, although how it was enforced in the domestic setting is difficult to imagine. It stated that no meal which began between the hours of 6pm and 9.30pm should consist of more than 3 courses. No meal which began at any other time should consist of more than 2 courses. Plain cheese was not regarded as a course. An hors d'oeuvre (not containing meat, fish, poultry or game), a dessert (consisting only of raw or dried fruit) and soup (not containing meat, fish, poultry or game) should be regarded as 'half a course'.

David Lloyd George had long been concerned about the abuse of alcohol, famously declaring that Britain had two enemies: Germany and Drink, and of the two Drink was the worse! So now both the selling and consumption of alcohol were restricted. Claims that war production was being hampered by drunkenness led to pub opening hours and even alcohol strength being reduced. Where they had previously been allowed to open all day, the new opening times were to be 12 noon until 2.30pm and 6.30 to 9.30pm – another measure that lasted way beyond the end of the war. Also a 'no treating' order made it an offence to buy drinks for others! As there were a number of pubs in Laugharne this would have had an effect on drinking habits, but anyone thinking they could get away with drinking out of hours was greatly mis-taken, for in those days Laugharne had its own Police Constable, George Henry Warmington, and the police station was situated in Market Street. PC Warmington made several successful prosecutions relating to drinking during prohibited hours, even including that of the local magistrate, J.D. Morse, who was fined one shilling for drinking whisky at 4.00pm one afternoon, in the Cross House Inn on the Grist! The licensee, Richard McConnell, who was in hospital at the time having been wounded whilst serving in the army, was also summonsed to appear. Mrs McConnell being the landlady in her husband's absence was called as a witness, but the case against the licensee was dismissed.

Tea was becoming ever more popular, particularly 'Typhoo' tea which was sold as 'the tea that doctors recommend' and was stocked by chemist shops, with its medicinal qualities ascribed to the purity of its leaf-edge tea. During the war the Government bought up all the available tea and distributed limited amounts to retailers at a fixed price. Typhoo could not be made from Gov-ernment tea, but requests for the supply of leaf-edge tea were turned down and an appeal by 400 medical professionals ignored. Typhoo customers then wrote to the 'Tea Controller' in great numbers claiming Typhoo tea was a

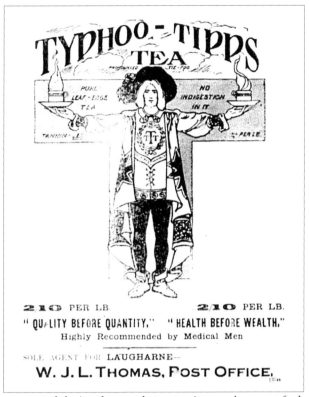

Tea: promoted during the war, but not quite a replacement for beer!

medical necessity. He eventually relented and gave permission for Typhoo to trade in leaf-edge tea throughout the war. In Laugharne the Chemist, Mr Ladd Thomas, was the sole agent for Typhoo and duly advertised in *The Welshman*. Tea was one of the commodities which would become rationed in 1918.

For the previous Christmas the Township had sent Christmas parcels of biscuits, cake, tobacco or cigarettes, tea tablets, peppermints, chocolate and a pair of mittens to those in the Mediterranean expeditionary forces. This year 80 Christmas parcels containing a tin of sweets, a cake, peppermints, a tablet of soap, towel, bootlaces, handkerchief and a Christmas card signed by the Portreeve, William E, Edwards, were sent. At home a few local philanthropists, including Mr J.D. Morse, Mrs Hurt, Mrs Peel and Mrs Matthew, kindly distributed gifts in kind and cash to several deserving poor.

The numerous festivities which had taken place over the Christmas period – football and rugby matches, fox hunts and concerts – had raised morale throughout the county, but the mood was soon dejected again. The loss of so many men on the Somme during 1916 had necessitated lowering the call-up age from 18 years 7 months, to 18 years. Despite union resistance every colliery in Britain received notices that more colliers were required for the army. The conditions for the colliers' call up are shown in the panel.

> 1. *Those who have entered the mines since 14 August 1915.*
> 2. *Surface workers or officials supervising such workers as enginemen, pumpmen, weighmen, electricians, fitters and mechanics.*
> 3. *Workers of military age employed in the mines who during the last three months had lost on an average two or more shifts during the week from avoidable causes.*

Local War Agricultural Committees introduced controls on certain basic commodities and began setting maximum prices for them. This was rationing of a sort, but it meant that those who could afford to pay the prices, did so, and those who could not pay went without, making it an unfair system. Potatoes were, of course, a staple in the diet of the majority of people at this time and this part of Carmarthenshire, along with Pembrokeshire, was known for its cultivation of early varieties. However, potato disease caused a shortage, which escalated into a crisis by the spring of 1917 due to the harsh winter, with tons of potatoes being frozen in the ground.

1917

At the end of January those newly eligible 18 year olds were beginning to be called up for service, with posters put up around Carmarthenshire (see panel).

> *Youths born in 1898 and 1899, who attested and were then trans-ferred to the Army Reserve. Those in Group A, born in 1898, are required to report themselves 15 days from the date of this Proclamation (January 30th); and men in Group B, born in 1899, 30 days from the date on which they attain 18 years of age.*
>
> *Youths deemed to be Reservists under the Military Service Acts, 1916. These have been assigned to classes according to the year of their birth and men of Class A, born in 1898, are required to report for the purpose of joining the Colours within 15 and 30 days respectively of January 30th.*

The War Office also declared it was necessary to call up half those men engaged in agriculture to whom tribunals had refused a certificate of exemption from military service. Arrangements would be made for several thousand men to be at the disposal of farmers. Again, in June 1917 the War Office agreed not to take any more men for the army who were already employed on farms, but only to defer this until after the harvest. This conflict of interests between the War Office who required more and more men to fight at the front, and the Board of Agriculture, who needed more farm workers to produce food for the country, continued right up until the last few months of the war.

Another appeal was placed in the local newspaper from the Vegetable Products Committee for more vegetables. By now there were branches at Laugharne and Llanstephan as well as Carmarthen and up until the end of December, when the depot had only been open for 3 months, they had sent 43 packages of vegetables to the North Sea Fleet, amounting to about 2 tons. The appeal was for one vegetable item a week from everyone with a garden and for every farmer coming to market the following Saturday to give one root vegetable each week. By October 1917 the Carmarthen branch, which included Laugharne and Llanstephan, had completed its first year's work and had sent off just under 4 tons of vegetables and fruit to the Grand Fleet. It was noted that Laugharne and Llanstephan had contributed their fair share of this and numerous letters of thanks from commanders of HM ships had been received by the committee.

Back in France, two more men with links to Laugharne were killed during February: Private Arthur Goring Thomas, of the 2nd South Wales Borderers (SWB), was killed on 4th February. His parents are buried in Laugharne church-yard. On the following day Private Robert Craig David, of the 49th Battalion, Australian Imperial Force (AIF), was killed near Bernafay Wood. His parents had migrated from Laugharne to Australia in the 1880s.

Although the majority of people in Laugharne seem to have fared quite well with regard to food, there were signs that some struggled to obtain what they needed. Between April 1916 and February 1917 a series of robberies involving food was reported in *The Welshman*. 100 eggs were stolen from the creamery. Thefts of both fowl and eggs were described as 'rampant' in the district – one farmer lost 14 fowl in two weeks. Other individual families also lost chickens and eggs. Cows were being milked in the night and sheep mysteriously disappeared. These robberies may have been committed by those unable to buy the food they needed, or by those planning to sell it on. Finally PC Warmington caught someone red-handed stealing coal and garden produce during the night, after which there were no more reported thefts.

Food was beginning to get scarce in Britain, with warnings of a forthcoming potato shortage and that strict regulations regarding foodstuffs were being considered. David Lloyd George even took the step of writing to the farmers of Britain, imploring them to keep food production levels up and informing them of a plan to bring extra labour into the market by moving men and women from other industries into land work to help the farmers. Local officials looked into utilising waste land around the county. During a heated debate at a meeting of county councillors on 31st January, one member of the committee, W.N. Jones, spoke of a suggestion to punish farmers who did not make full use of their land. Mervyn Peel sided with the farmers, who were struggling for labourers. However Nathan Griffiths, also a member of the Carmarthenshire Military Tribunal, accused farmers of sending their sons to work in reserved occupations to evade military service and said that farmers were better off now than they had ever been due to the increased price of food.

In February 1917 during the potato crisis there were reports of a scene at Carmarthen Market when the farmers who brought their potatoes to market were ordered to sell them at the Food Controller's maximum price of £8 per ton, plus carriage of between sixpence and one shilling. The previous week's price had been £13 a ton. Inevitably there was a scramble of customers when farmers began to sell at the new price and a scene ensued for a few minutes until order was restored!

Cinemas around the county were playing the latest films which had been released following the success of *The Battle of the Somme*; namely *The Advance of the Tank* and *The Battle of the Ancre*. These films proved immensely popular and cinemas around the county regularly played these to full houses.

At the St Clears Licensing Sessions on Tuesday, 13th February, Superintendent J.E. Jones stated that there were 41 licensed premises in the district (which included Laugharne and Llanstephan). The population in the area was 5,083 which meant that there was a pub to every 121 inhabitants. St Clear's village itself had 20 public houses and a population of 1,250, making one pub for every 62 inhabitants. Concluding his speech, the Superintendent recommended cancellation of the renewal of licenses for several public houses; the Rose and Crown, Chemical Inn, Gardde Arms and New Inn at St Clears and the Ship & Castle at Laugharne. The Ship & Castle was, of course, owned by William Griffith who also ran Brown's, directly across the road. The Chairman of the committee pointed out that the public houses served not just the community but were a vital focal point for fairs around the district, where goods were bought and sold. The Superintendent pointed out that fairs were dying out and local marts were becoming the norm. A resolution was passed to leave things be, but warn any licensees who had been convicted of any offences about their future conduct. A special meeting was agreed upon, to take place on 22nd March. Tudor Williams, a motor garage proprietor of Laugharne and St Clears appeared in court that day, charged with falsifying documents relating to several purchases of gasoline in order to evade duty. Williams was fined £5 17s for his misdemeanour.

A number of local men were home on leave in Laugharne during the month, including Private John John, of Gosport; Private William Richards, of Church Farm; and Private William John, of the 4th Welsh. Another military visitor, coming to see the birthplace of his mother and to visit her family, was a soldier of the New Zealand Expeditionary Force, Sergeant Gwynne Clayton Brewer. His mother, Margaret Rogers, of Malt House Farm, had emigrated to New Zealand with her parents and siblings during the 1880s and had married Gwynne's father in 1887. Her father, Reverend Griffith Jones, was a clergyman who had made the decision to take his family out to the fledgling country.

News was received that Private Merlin Rees Watts, of the Monmouth Regiment, was in hospital in Brecon, after falling seriously ill, while Lieutenant Thomas Lewis Ebsworth, 6th Welsh, of The Beach Hotel, Pendine, wrote a lengthy letter to his mother describing the latest action he had been involved in, and asked her to tell the parents of Private Ben Evans, of Lasfach Farm, Laugharne, that he had been among the first people he had met during a recent advance and the two of them had enjoyed a cheerful reunion on the battlefield! The parents of Driver John Thomas, Royal Field Artillery, received a letter at their home at Castletoch Farm, describing how his gun battery had been speedily following up the German withdrawal on the Somme and was presently sited in a field of wheat which 'had been sown by the huns'… Driver William Adams, Royal Field Artillery, of Brixtarw, also wrote home with similar news.

All over the country two systems had been in operation for selling bread. One was by weight, the price varying with the market, the other was the assize system in which if the price of flour went up the baker reduced the weight of the loaf and told the customer. This was no longer to be the case: in February it was declared that bread was to be sold only by weight. Every loaf must be either 2lbs or 4lbs. A few months later bread was in short supply, due to the worldwide failure of the harvest in 1916 and people were encouraged to eat 1lb a week less. In April 1917 it was reported in *The Welshman* that people in Swansea and Cardiff were now paying 1s for a 4lb loaf, but that folk in Laugharne had been paying that for the previous 3 weeks! In June there was a movement to establish a cooperative bakery in Laugharne with a view to supplying bread at reasonable prices and re-starting the Grist Mill for grinding local corn was also contemplated. But before anything could be done, at the end of September the price of a 4lb loaf was fixed at 9d, which was a welcome reduction.

In March 1917 there was a report in the local press about a scramble for sugar in St Clears. It was said to be bought, not by the poor, who couldn't afford it, but by the comparatively well-off. A large consignment arrived in St Clears and was being sold at 6 shillings for 14lbs, and was soon sold out. Consumption of sugar had been set at ¾lb per head and shops were only selling 1lb or ½lb at a time. This only served to highlight the inequality in food distribution and it was suggested that the German ticket system for food would be better than this. The feeling was that 'if there is a shortage of food, let us all suffer alike'.

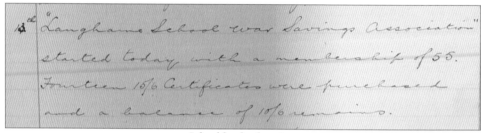

School log book entry.

Mr Tyler's father, Samuel, had died in December 1916, aged 81, but Mr Tyler continued to expand his own support of the war effort. In March he helped form a War Savings Association based at the school but open to everyone, and he took on the role of Secretary. The school children were also still collecting eggs on Tuesdays each week, with nearly 450 in total being sent in during April alone.

By April female labour in the fields and gardens was becoming a common sight, but nevertheless still attracted condescending newspaper comments. *The Welshman* reported that in Laugharne several women were assisting farmers, and that 'females galore' were cultivating gardens.

> ### The Welshman: 20th April, 1917
> *LAUGHARNE NOTES & NEWS. Women labour. Female labour is becoming a prominent feature in the district. Several women are assisting the farmers. Females galore are busy whenever the weather permits cultivating their gardens and plots of land and one day last week one of the fairer sex was seen busily assisting in the felling of timber, handling the saw with tact and energy.*

The outbreak of war had led to a great increase in mechanisation in farming across the UK as a whole, although the less wealthy farmers of Carmarthenshire had been slower to respond to this leap forward in technology. However, the pressure on farmers to achieve even more with fewer employees continued and so they became increasingly interested in mechanisation. D. Bradbury Jones, of the West Wales Garage, Carmarthen, began an expensive advertising campaign throughout Carmarthenshire during the month, splashing advertisements for 'The Overtime Farm Tractor' for which he had just become sole agent and stockist in Carmarthenshire. His advertising centred on the fact that even a farm girl could handle the tractor! The condescending tone was typical of the time – but at least it signalled one small step on the way toward recognition of female workers.

Captain Thomas Jones of Grove House, Laugharne, received the welcome news from Singapore that his son, Jeremiah Whittaker Jones, an engineer aboard the SS *Tantalus*, was safe and well. His ship was a passenger ship which sailed to far eastern destinations from London and which, oddly, was sold to Germany after the war, in 1922. News also reached Laugharne that three local men: Corporal John Williams, Royal Engineers, of the Corporation Arms; Private William Roberts, 4th Welsh, of Gosport; and Private William John of The Butts, had met up in Egypt while enjoying some well-deserved leave in Cairo. A large number of local soldiers and sailors were home on leave during the month, but some concern was raised due to the lack of news about Private William Howells, of Woodreef, Marros, who had been missing since March. Sergeant David Owen Thomas, Canadian Infantry, son of Reverend John Thomas, of Laugharne, had also returned home on leave following a spell in hospital recovering from wounds suffered during the famous Canadian assault on Vimy Ridge in April. He had spent five weeks in hospital and returned to Laugharne with a backpack which had saved his life, showing his parents the eight bullet holes in it and a breadknife which had stopped a potentially fatal bullet!

In 1917 came another demand for an increase in agricultural production due to the widespread failure of potato crops due to disease. It had not affected the local crop quite so badly as it was reportedly 'satisfactory'. Colonel Bolton offered to supply seed potatoes at a fixed price and, by May, the planting of potatoes was well under way in the district and the increase in acreage was considerable.

By May there was no longer enough feed to keep poultry and pigs, and so that was now discouraged, with the exception of hens, in order for them to keep laying eggs, but not as meat for the table.

In June 1917 the 'Sugar Commission' made sugar available to private fruit growers who wished to preserve their own fruit by making jam on their own premises for domestic consumption. The Commission could only guarantee to supply as long as stocks were available. As for housewives who wished to preserve fruit, the Board of Agriculture sent out representatives to give talks and demonstrations on fruit bottling and preserving *without* sugar. One such talk took place in the Infants school in Laugharne at the end of July 1917 and was well attended.

During the quarterly meeting of the Carmarthenshire Joint Standing Committee in July pleasing statistics showed 200 fewer crimes throughout the county compared to the previous year. Mr W. Picton-Philipps spoke at length about casualties amongst the county police officers who were serving in the forces. There was still some concern about the possibility of enemy agents in the county and Mervyn Peel asked Picton-Philipps for the number of aliens in the county. He was told that there were:

> 376 adults and 264 children; 5 Austrians, 16 Germans, 3 Hungarians, 3 Turks, 124 Belgians, 17 French, 60 Italians, 9 Portuguese, 99 Russians, 15 Americans, 3 Romanians, 2 Danes, 3 Dutch, 2 Norwegians, 1 Spanish, 10 Swedes, 1 Swiss and 3 other nationalities.

There was also a number of enemy aliens unaccounted for in the county as well as some who had resided there for many years and who had become naturalised.

During the month there were pleasing reports of the harvest from farmers all around the county, who were now receiving help with their crops from recuperating soldiers and women, but this was tempered with news of an outbreak of typhus at Kidwelly, where over 40 people had been taken ill and eight had died by the end of July.

By early August 1917 an outbreak of potato disease in the West Country was reportedly spreading north. Wart disease appeared in some crops in Carmarthenshire and blight was reported in St Clears. That summer, early signs were that the harvest would be satisfactory, but by the end of August *The Carmarthen Journal* reported that:

> ...the month would be remembered as one of the most remarkable months of the year for weather conditions. West Wales experiencing abnormally wet weather and agriculturalists were alarmed at the condition of the crops as a result of continuous rain for the previous 3 weeks.

In August 1917 Mr Tyler took up the matter of establishing funds to support 'a proper reception to "our boys" when they come home on a visit or otherwise'.

Also in the newspapers on 7th September was the sad news of the funeral of a young girl from Laugharne, Florence Martha Richards, who died at Haverfordwest on 1st September. Her mother, Mary Ann Richards, was the daughter of a well-known fishing family, the Browns. Her husband, James Richards, whom she had met in Haverfordwest whilst working for a Mr Williams, was serving in the Middle East with the Hampshire Regiment and had never seen his daughter. She had been born in December 1915 after he had sailed for Egypt. The sad death of her child was a terrible blow to Mary, yet within three months she also received a letter which dealt her a further crippling blow (see panel). After the war Mary married her cousin George Brown and one of the couple's children, Glynford Brown, served during World War II alongside three other Laugharne men in 1st Commando.

Dear Mrs Richards,—please accept my deepest sympathy with you in your sad bereavement. As I have been nursing your husband, Pte. J. Richards (2/5th Hamps), and was with him when he died I thought perhaps it might help you just a little to have some particulars about him. He was admitted to this hospital on December 3rd suffering from dysentery. On Wednesday evening it was found he had an appendix abscess which required immediate operation and he was transferred to this ward shortly after midnight from the operating theatre. He was very ill indeed, but by morning was considerably better. On Friday he had a very comfortable night and slept well and was quite bright on Saturday morning when I left him. In the afternoon he took worse and had a lot of pain. He was very ill when I came on duty on Saturday night. Everything that could be done to save him had been done, but without success. He seemed to decide in his own mind that he would not recover, but it did not appear to trouble him. When I asked him for a message for you, he said, 'I love my wife so much until death', to which I answered, 'In death ye are not divided'. He had very little pain the last night and passed quietly away shortly after midnight on Sunday, December 9th. He was conscious until about ten minutes before the end. The Congregational chaplain was with him about 12.30, having previously visited him during the day. Your husband asked me to have his testament buried with him. I found amongst his belongings a khaki New

Testament which had been presented him by the Congregational Church, Haverfordwest. Presuming that was what he referred to, I put it with his remains. There seems to be very little that we can do here to compensate you women in England for being unable to visit your loved ones when they are sick, but of course the distance to Egypt prevents anyone visiting here. Again assuring you of my sympathy in your sorrow and with kind regards, I remain, yours truly, M. Buchanan, Staff Nurse.

Militancy was spreading from the coalfields and woollen mills to the other working trades throughout September. A meeting of Carmarthen Town Council during the month debated the election of Labour Councillors, and local workers in the town demanded more war bonuses. Military Appeals Tribunals through-out the county worked flat out to work through the hundreds of appeals from civilians who did not wish to go to war and local dairy farmers were threat-ened with imprisonment for selling milk at higher prices than the Government allowed.

Back in Laugharne school Mr Tyler urged the school children to collect conkers for the war effort, although it was never explained to schoolchildren exactly what the conkers would do! Nor did they care. They were more inter-ested in the War Office's bounty of 7s 6d (37.5p) for every hundredweight they handed in. 7/6 is equivalent to around £23 today!

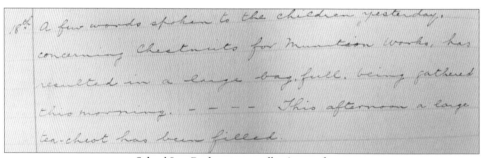

School Log Book entry – collecting conkers.

Over the country the children's efforts were so successful that they collected more conkers than there were trains to transport them, and piles were seen rotting at railway stations. But a total of 3,000 tonnes of conkers did reach their destination – the Synthetic Products Company at top-secret factories at Holton Heath in Dorset and King's Lynn in Norfolk. Altogether around 3,000 tonnes of conkers were collected by Britain's children in 1917. They were used to make acetone, a vital component of the smokeless propellant for shells and bullets known as cordite. Before the war the acetone used in British munitions had been made almost entirely in the US from distilling birch and it arrived in the UK on ships.

The massive increase in shell production for the war meant the country had to find a UK-based source of acetone as, by 1915, its shortage had caused a critical shortage of shells. The British Government's response was to create a dedicated Ministry of Munitions, run by the future Prime Minister David Lloyd George. One of his first initiatives was to ask Dr Chaim Weizmann (a chemist working at Manchester University) if there was an alternative way of making acetone in large quantities. Through experimentation, Dr Weizmann originally obtained acetone from grains, potatoes and other starchy foods. But by 1917, as grain and potatoes were needed to feed the British population and the armed forces, and German U-boat activity in the Atlantic was threatening to cut off the import of maize from the United States, Weizmann was tasked to find another supply of starch for his process that would not interfere with the already limited food supplies. His work led to conkers being used instead! Dr Weizmann went on to become the first President of Israel after its foundation in 1948!

Posters were put up in schools, encouraging children to gather conkers. Boy Scout leaders helped organise collections.

Sadly, the plan wasn't a great success.

In Laugharne local people tried to continue life much as before the war. However, there were some differences, as photos of carnival floats illustrate.

Laugharne Carnival float.

This photo of a float was taken, it is believed, around the start of the war. Many horses had been requisitioned for the war effort, but fortunately donkeys were used by Laugharne cocklers and so were available, in place of horses, to pull the float cart.

During October the Women's Army Auxiliary Corps (WAAC) published a series of articles which pressed the need for women to enlist into their corps. A well-attended meeting took place at County Hall at Carmarthen, which made the call for: orderly clerks, shorthand typists, accountants, librarians, cooks, waitresses, housemaids, vegetable women, pantry maids, laundresses, wine waitresses, cleaners, storehouse women, driver-mechanics etc. Among the local women in the WAAC was Miss Jane Brown, of The Grist, whose brother George William Brown had been severely wounded earlier in the war. She had completed her training and was about to embark for France.

A sense of the passion with which much of the population still wished to support the war effort can be read from the outrage shown in the newspaper cutting (see panel) at the very thought that anyone could possibly consider support for Germany.

> **The Carmarthen Weekly Reporter – 9th November, 1917**
> *A German document which has just been published speaks of information supplied by "One of our Agents at Cardiff". We must not rashly assume that the agent was a German. One of the most extraordinary facts which has come to light in the spy trials is that there are English people who work against our country for German gold.*

Support for the war, however, did not prevent local miners from going out on strike as a protest against the owners of the Gwaun-Cae-Gurwen Colliery. They were concerned that the return of soldiers after the war would force down wages and they had begun their battle to ensure that this would not occur. Several meetings then took place in the Amman Valley during the month to discuss the matter. The miners had recently accepted another pay rise of 1s. 6d. per day and the price of coal was raised by 2s. 6d. per ton to cover the increased wages. Soldiers and sailors who were putting their lives on the line had also been awarded 1s. a day extra pay for each year's service! Strikes continued intermittently throughout the South Wales collieries over the coming weeks.

News was received in Laugharne that Gunner Tom Harry, Clifton Street, had been wounded in France (see chapter three for more about him). Mr and Mrs

Renfrey, of Brook School, received an interesting letter from their son, Fred Renfrey, an air mechanic with the Royal Flying Corps, who told them of a 400 mile flight over enemy lines, and a number of military visitors were enjoying a spell of leave in the Township. A Reception Committee, first proposed by Mr Tyler, was finally formed in Laugharne during November to organise collections and welcome home receptions for troops on leave, which would include all those from Laugharne Township and Parish, Llansadurnen and Llandawke. Mrs Bolton and Mrs Mordaunt-Smith were two prominent members of the committee.

Even with the campaign in the Middle East turning in favour of the Allies, there was a desperate shortage of oil in Britain due to enemy submarine activity. With the onset of winter, people around Carmarthenshire found they were having to walk miles to locate stocks of paraffin for heating and lighting, and were frequently stuck in queues which were worse than those for food – the shortage of oil would continue until the end of the war. Butter, too, was reported to be 'almost unobtainable at present'.

Local newspapers throughout the county filled their pages with photographs and articles of the fallen and, as another traumatic year drew to a close, figures suggest that 1,918 men from Carmarthenshire had fallen, 19 of whom were either from Laugharne or had family in the Township. The separate Palestine and Mesopotamian campaigns had recovered from early setbacks; and the two expeditionary forces were gaining ground from the Turks. The Salonika campaign threatened to become active once Greece finally declared war on Germany. The war at sea was at a stalemate, with heavy losses amongst merchant shipping, due to the U-boat campaign; and the three main offensives on the Western Front had, at best, not lived up to expectations. Food shortages affected morale in Britain, but in Germany things were even worse, as the Royal Navy's stranglehold on the seas had virtually cut supplies to Germany. There was militancy from miners, railwaymen and munitions workers in Britain, but the German civil population was also on the verge of mutiny. The Italian army was on the brink of collapse after a disastrous set of offensives and it had then been sent reeling by a German and Austrian offensive at Caporetto in November. Britain and France had sent troops there to bolster Italy's defence.

A large number of local men had the good fortune to be given leave over Christmas and spent precious time at home with their families. Most of the newspaper columns were filled with tales of returned servicemen, along with news of several who had been awarded gallantry medals during the fighting over the previous months. Concerts were held all around the county to cele-brate the safe return home of local heroes, many of whom were presented with personal items, ranging from purses of money to items such as engraved watches, snuff boxes and cigarette cases. However, as the New Year opened, the good fortune of having sons and husbands at home for Christmas was tempered by the continued reports in the newspapers of fresh casualties, whilst the introduction of meat rationing would add to the anguish felt by the civilian population.

In December 1917 it was reported that butter was unobtainable in Laugharne. A supply of margarine arrived that month but was soon sold out. Meat figured then much more in family diets than today, and each year *The Welshman* described the quality and quantity of meat on display in the butcher's shops in Laugharne and every time it seemed to be:

> even better than in previous years... judging by appearances there were not many meatless days in Laugharne over the holiday.

However, at Christmastime it became very apparent that some families could not afford to buy food, especially meat. Every year throughout the war a distri-bution of gifts in cash and kind to the poor was made. Most often this was provided by the local gentry who were named as Mr J.D. Morse, Mrs Hurt, Mrs Peel, Major and Mrs Matthew, Mrs Stark, Rev. Thomas, Mrs Davies, Mr A.W. Thomas, Miss E. Falkener and Captain T. Jones. At Christmas 1917 Mr W.H. Dempster sent a cheque to the vicar requesting it to be spent on meat for those in need and Mrs Harrison also sent a cheque with the request that coal be supplied to a list of persons mentioned. The names of the recip-ients were not recorded.

December also saw the first war memorial erected in the church: a beautiful brass tablet to Lionel Mordaunt-Smith, who had been killed in France in May. The following April was to see a beautiful glass case installed in the entrance to St Martin's Church with a Roll of Honour of the 26 'Laugharne boys who have fallen in this terrible War'. It might as well have added 'So far'!

At the end of 1917 and during January 1918, the Western Division of the Carmarthen Union District Committee of the Carmarthenshire Executive Agricultural Committee met to consider objections by farmers against the cultivation orders recently served upon them. Under the chairmanship of Mr G.O. Lewis of East House Farm, Laugharne, nearly 460 cases were dealt with in 7 sittings. Mr Lewis was praised for the way in which he conducted proceedings. The cultivation order for the West Division, in which Laugharne's farms lay, demanded an increase of 68% over and above the acreage cultivated in 1916. This was a huge increase given the shortage of labour, but farmers recognised the importance of increasing the food supply. However, at the same time they had concerns over security of tenure and the prices they received. Nevertheless, they responded to the demand and in January 1918 at a farmers' meeting it was unanimously decided to purchase a steam threshing machine for the district as the only local thresher was unable to cope with all the work in such a large district. In addition to working the land there was also a movement to further improve the local livestock.

On 28th February, 1918 there was another meeting of the farmers' union with the intention of forming a branch to represent the Township together with Llansadurnen and Llandawke. 59 members enrolled immediately, including some women, who were also eligible to join. Farmers and smallholders in Laugharne and Pendine were urged to increase the production of potatoes and to raise pigs in order to aid the war effort.

In Laugharne itself better news had been received by James Adams, of Gosport Street, who heard from his son Corporal Thomas Adams, of the 11th Royal Fusiliers, that he had been recommended for the Distinguished Conduct Medal. The citation for his award, which is second only to the Victoria Cross, was published in the press (see panel). Compare the citation to that of Corporal

---

***London Gazette* of 10 January 1918:**
'For conspicuous gallantry and devotion to duty as stretcher-bearer in an attack. He carried wounded men from the thickest part of the enemy barrage to the aid post and worked un-ceasingly throughout the day and the following night dressing and bringing in wounded. His conduct is worthy of the highest praise.'

William Charles Fuller, VC, of Laugharne early in the war, when he was awarded the Victoria Cross for rescuing just one man, an officer, and it is easy to see that Laugharne could have been home to two winners of the highest award for valour.

While the miners were worried about their wages and future job security, farmers around the county were reporting that the good start to the harvest had been ruined by the wet weather which hit the country during August and September, the same weather which had turned the Flanders battlefield into mud.

In January 1918 Carmarthenshire stood third in the list of Welsh counties for the number of local women working on the land. By June the Women's Land Service Corps, which had been formed in early 1916, were overwhelmed with demands for women to hoe and weed. Volunteers were asked to join weeding gangs immediately, and for not less than 4 to 6 weeks' duration. The minimum wage was £1 a week and reduced rail fares were allowed to the place of work. It is not known how many young women from Laugharne joined this Land Service Corps, but Miss C. Thomas of Clifton Street was one of them, returning home to Laugharne in June 1919.

The hard reality of war was felt in the county when a lifeboat containing the body of a sailor washed ashore at Laugharne on 8th February. Two months later another boat washed ashore at Lacques Farm, Llanstephan, containing the badly decomposed body of yet another sailor.

Children continued to help the war effort and during a special local 'children's week' the following enthusiastic helpers sold stamps: Amy Harries; Beatrice Lewis; Doris John; May and Jennie Phillips; Laura Thomas; May and Polly McConnell; Millie Francis; Mary Wright; Edith John; Maggie Pearce; Annie Hancock; B. Lewis; Chas Beynon; and Reggie and Arthur Adams.

The schools were closed on Thursday last that day being set apart to herald the coming of food rationing. Mr R.H. Tyler headmaster with the whole of his staff were busy from 9am to 6pm preparing the food cards for this area, which were duly delivered at each house on Friday morning.

The school was also involved in March 1918 when food rationing came to Laugharne. The Government took control of the food supply by introducing a national system of rationing, so the ration books needed to be distributed.

In Laugharne preparation of the ration cards fell to the Headmaster, Mr Tyler, and his staff. The schools were closed for the day on Thursday 21st March while the cards were prepared and they were duly delivered to each house the following day by the postman. An individual weekly ration was a maximum of 1oz of tea, and 4oz of butter or margarine, dependent on stocks available and it could sometimes be less! A week later meat was also rationed. In August the meat coupons were even required when purchasing poultry or rabbits at market. By October the meat ration for the winter was set at 1s 4d worth for the week, although hams and bacon were coupon-free and the fat ration was increased to 6oz of butter or margarine and 2oz of lard. The sugar ration remained unchanged. Jam was also rationed to 4oz for adults and 6oz for children. The non-rationed foods were bread, vegetables and cheese. There was also a general lack of fruit. At Christmas time coupons were required for poultry, but could be combined. One coupon would get a bird of up to 3lb weight, two coupons up to 5lbs and three coupons above 5lbs. On November 2nd the first ration books expired and new books were issued which would last 26 weeks. These consisted of blue and green sheets for meat, brown for lard, light blue for butter and margarine, yellow for sugar, plus spare coupons which might be required for jam. A grey sheet was included and this would be used in due course for applying for the third ration book, which meant the ration books continued in use almost to the end of 1919, so the effects of the war continued well beyond the peace agreement.

On 1st March *The Carmarthen Journal* reported on a meeting of Laugharne farmers which took place at Bwlchnewydd, where it was decided to form a branch of the Farmers' Union in the parish and not to amalgamate with the Township. It was agreed that farmers ran a bigger risk than most of suffering financially due to the vagaries of the weather. Where they paid trade union rates to their staff for the hours they worked and received Government rates of interest on their capital, food would still be dearer, but as long as a farmer could pay his rent and rates he would be satisfied. Those elected to serve on the committee were; T. Howells, Castle Lloyd (Treasurer); William Bowen, Cwmbrwyn (Secretary); David James, West Mead (delegate to the County conference); Messrs Evans, Croesland; Evan Benjamin, Great Hill; Thomas D. Rees, Great Bishop's Court; Mr Matthias, Brook; H. Howells, Castle Lloyd; John Rees Johns, Brixton; H. Evans, Woodhouse; Thomas Rees, Cross Inn; Thomas Jenkins, Maesygrove and Thomas Skeel Morse Jnr, Maesgwrda.

In May, the teachers of Carmarthenshire also went on strike in protest about their pay. An assistant teacher in the county earned little more than £2 a week, while a colliery labourer could now expect to earn £3 to £4 per week. A meeting at Pontyberem held early in the month discussed the pay of teachers at Llanelli, who were paid more than teachers in the rest of the county. Members of the Labour Party were in attendance to support the teachers' demands, which probably helped to further diminish local support of the Liberal Party, whose popularity in their one-time heartland was dwindling fast. To add insult to injury, a week later the calling up of teachers into the army began. While the Carmarthenshire teachers remained out on strike during June, miners at Tirydail decided to strike at the beginning of the month. Almost 600 men laid down their tools in protest at the sacking of some of their fellow workers. The owners, Cleeve's Western Anthracite, re-instated the men and the colliers went back to work.

On 20th May, a German prisoner of war, Franz Sauter, escaped from a camp at Llandybie. The man was a fluent English speaker and he made his way to Grovesend, hoping to steal a boat at Swansea. He was caught by the police within two days. On the same day that Sauter escaped, thousands of people from the area assembled around the Town Hall in Laugharne, to enjoy the fun of the Common Walk, which takes place every third year. The walk, also known as the 'Beating of the Bounds', was led by Tom John, a miner who had returned to Laugharne from Abergwynfi especially for the occasion. After breakfast in the streets, the assembly started off from the Grist at 7.00am for their day of fun, which saw them walk the twenty-plus mile boundary of Laugharne. The main party returned to Laugharne by 4.00pm, and, after confirming that the boundaries had not been encroached upon, then the local pubs were drunk dry. Nothing has changed in Laugharne!

A large number of local soldiers were on leave in Laugharne during the month, among them Private Benjamin Alfred Roblin, of the Australian Machine Gun Corps. The son of James and Mary Roblin, of Colston Farm, he had been a Policeman before migrating to Australia in 1913 to live at Mossdale, New South Wales. This was the first time he had been home to visit his parents in five years. He returned to Australia after the war and he died on 31st July, 1970. Two of his brothers, Arthur James and Herbert Roblin, were also serving at the front.

Corporal John Raymond, in Egypt with the 24th Welsh, wrote home to his parents at Delacorse to tell them that the heat in Palestine had affected his health to the extent that he had been forced to transfer away from the infantry to the Transport section at Ludd – not altogether bad news!

In May the Ministry of Food said that too much imported butter was coming into the Carmarthen Rural district and a reduction would have to be made. Asked why imported butter should be sent to Laugharne, the reply was that all the milk there was sold and that none went into the making of butter. However, cheese production had just recommenced at the milk factory in Broadway. Gloucester, Cheddar and other cheeses were being made, so there must have been some surplus milk available for that.

Whilst local farmers were being pressed to produce more and more, they were also still being pressed to do so with less labour. In June the Army Council wanted 30,000 more men from farms for army service. The men were to be provided through the local War Agricultural Committees by quota, with no appeals to the tribunals, except on grounds of conscience or exceptional hardship. All agricultural exemptions were abolished. The places of the men called up were to be filled by an additional 10,000 German prisoners and by employing more women on the land. The Carmarthen Farmers' Union called for the postponement of calling up young farm workers and the local MP, Mr John Hinds, asked in Parliament for the call-up to be deferred until end of June, to enable farmers to make other arrangements. A deputation of farmers from Carmarthenshire went up to London to protest against the quota of 590 men to be taken from the county, whereas Pembrokeshire was asked to supply only 350 men. The farmers believed it to be essential to retain the few skilled men left on farms as most farms were then working with the minimum of labour available to them, and the more land that was cultivated would mean food would be destroyed for lack of labour to harvest the crops. At a meeting of the War Cabinet in late June it was finally decided not to call up any more farm hands until after the harvest. Carmarthen War Agricultural Committee sent a telegram to the Food Production Department asking for call-up notices already issued to be suspended. This matter was again raised in Parliament, where it was decided that any call-up notices issued before 26th June would actually be enforced.

Land workers throughout the county had been called up during June and, at a meeting of the Carmarthenshire Farmer's Union on 8th June, the figure of 1,000 workers called up in the county was reported to the large crowd in attendance. However, this was later revised down to 500. The timing could not have been worse, as harvest time was about to begin and labour was needed to bring in the crops. In July, Carmarthen War Agricultural Committee announced certain categories of men could be exempted from military service if they volunteered immediately for agricultural work. Farmers needing volunteers had to apply at once to be allocated volunteers from their own neighbourhood as far as possible. German POWs would also be sent out in escorted gangs. Thus by the end of August the harvest had been safely gathered in, helped by those female land workers.

The month also saw claims by county roadmen for an increase in wages. At a meeting of the Carmarthenshire Main Roads Committee the motion was passed to award the roadmen an extra three shillings. Meanwhile, the county teachers' strike was in its seventh week by 15th June, and there was no sign of an agreement being reached.

No doubt many of the strikers found time to visit Llanelli, where a British Mark I tank, named Julian, was on display throughout June to raise money. To allow the Government to borrow more money to help fund the Great War, War Bonds and Savings Certificates were introduced and businesses and members of the public were encouraged to invest to help the war effort. The tank had arrived on 10th June and was driven to the main entrance gates of the town hall, where it was parked up and opened up for three days for members of the public to look around it. The tank drew great crowds of people, who were fascinated by the giant 'landship' of which they had heard so much during its actions on the Somme and at Cambrai. Money was still being collected there on the Wednesday evening when the tank left for Carmarthen, and it was displayed at the Guildhall Square on Thursday 13th June. The total money raised in Wales during the first two weeks of the tour was an amazing £1,937,593.

> **The Welshman: 5th July, 1918**
> *LAUGHARNE NOTES & NEWS. The People's Bill.*
> *The new list of voters appeared in the porches of the respective places of worship on Sunday and there was much ado on account of so many ladies names appearing therein.*
> *Many were the threats of the fair sex at the dinner table "Now then for my vote next election".*

July saw the passing of a new Act of Parliament. Without it many of the men who had served in the war would not have been eligible to vote, and certainly none of the women. So the Act extended the vote to all men over the age of 21, but only to women over the age of 30 who held property worth £5 or more, or those who had husbands who did. It also introduced residency as the prerequisite for voting as well as the first-past-the-post system. So, once more, the war triggered practices that continued long into the future.

Meanwhile, at home, news of injury and loss continued to arrive. Mrs E. Lewis, Hugdon Cottage, received a letter from her gallant son, Gunner Frank Lewis, saying that he was in hospital suffering from having been gassed, though he cheerfully told his mother not to worry and that he hoped to be home soon. He did come home in July but then returned to Germany shortly to be incarcerated there as a POW! His story is told in chapter three.

While young men were falling on the battlefield, militancy was again the order of the day back at home. Farmers in Carmarthenshire campaigned against reduced hours of labour, and craftsmen and surface workers in the Amman, Dulais and Gwendraeth Valleys agitated for an eight-hour day, including meal breaks. The strike at Tirydail Colliery had been settled, but the teachers were still out, with 54 schools affected around the county.

Glowing reports of the advance in France were published daily and – at last – thoughts of a possible end to the war began to be contemplated by the population. Any very occasional sighting of an aircraft in the area was reported in the local press as it was such a rare spectacle, so when one actually landed in a field at Pendine after running short on fuel, it drew a large crowd of curious sightseers, before being refuelled and taking off again next morning.

In contrast to the previous year, this year's harvest was reportedly good, especially corn and wheat, with a record crop of oats produced. Potatoes and turnips also promised a fine yield.

When, in August 1918, a party of wounded soldiers from Carmarthen came to Laugharne, Mr Tyler again took a lead with the organisation of a major reception. In late August 1918 children were encouraged to collect nuts, acorns and beechmast to be used as pig food. It was emphasised that nuts were an important foodstuff to collect as, if gathered ripe, they could be shelled and stored in tins and the shells sent to the national collectors. The nutshells were then used to make charcoal to go inside anti-gas masks for the soldiers. If there was no local depot, people were advised that they could be sent carriage forward to the gasworks at Southend.

A 'blackberry order' had also come into force on 28th August, 1918, the aim of which was to produce as much jam as possible. The systematic collection of the fruit would be done by boy scouts, girl guides, school children and others up and down the country. 3d a pound would be paid to the pickers by local collection centres, of which there were about 100 in each county. Parcels of 5cwt and over would then be sent to jam manufacturers, who would pay 4½d per pound. If no transport was available locally to take the fruit to the collection centres then, in order that the fruit would not be wasted, it could be sold to the public at the fixed price of 4d per pound. The blackberries that year were reportedly a bumper crop:

> Never before has the blackberry been awarded so much distinction in the category of British fruit. It has come to the rescue in a period of extraordinary fruit shortage.

MISCELLANEOUS RECIPES.

Jugged Rabbit with Savoury Balls.—INGREDIENTS.—1½ lb. rabbit, 1 pint meat or vegetable stock, 1 oz. flour or fine oatmeal, 1½ oz. bacon fat or dripping, 1 peeled onion stuck with 3 cloves, grated rind of half a lemon, bacon trimmings, bunch of herbs, six allspice.

METHOD.—Soak the rabbit in tepid salted water for half an hour to free it from any blood. Then dry and cut into neat joints. Roll these in the flour. Heat the fat in the saucepan or casserole, lay in and fry the floured pieces of rabbit, add the stock, and stir gently until boiling. Next put in the onion, bacon bones and rinds, herbs, allspice, and lemon. Add a little seasoning, cover closely, and simmer in a cool oven, or on a low gas or fire, for about two and a half hours, or till the rabbit is tender and beginning to leave the bones. Time will therefore depend on the age of the rabbit. When ready, either serve in the casserole, or arrange the rabbit on a hot dish, and pour over the sauce. The onion and the herbs must either way be removed, the former being saved for future use. Place the balls round as a border, or serve in a separate dish.

The Savoury Balls.—INGREDIENTS.—3 oz. flour, 3 oz. fine oatmeal, 2 oz. chopped suet, 1 tablespoonful chopped onion, 2 teaspoonfuls chopped parsley, ¼ teaspoonful each salt and baking-powder, water to bind stiffly, seasoning.

METHOD.—Mix all these ingredients stiffly with water. Divide into six or twelve pieces, according to whether you wish one large or two small balls for each person, and shape like marbles. Roll each lightly in flour; then boil up the stew and add them three-quarters of an hour before serving. The gravy should just boil when they are added, and continue to boil for five minutes before lowering the heat, otherwise the balls lose their shape.

Marrow with Tomatoes.—INGREDIENTS.—1 marrow, 1 oz. of margarine, 1 heaped dessertspoonful of chopped parsley, 3 or 4 peppercorns, 4 or 5 tomatoes, 1 teaspoonful of cornflour, seasoning to taste.

METHOD.—Peel the marrow and cut into pieces about two inches big (removing the seeds, of course). Put these into a pan of boiling water with the peppercorns and a heaped teaspoonful of salt. Melt the margarine in a small pan, and stir in the flour smoothly; add the tomatoes, thinly sliced, and as much seasoning as you need. Stew these gently together, stirring well, to the consistency of sauce. When the marrow is tender, drain it carefully and place in a hot dish, and pour over it the tomato sauce into which you have stirred the parsley at the last minute. Serve very hot.

MISCELLANEOUS RECIPES.

Marrow au Gratin.—INGREDIENTS.—1 young marrow, ¼ pint milk and marrow stock, ½ oz. cornflour, 2 ozs. cheese, seasoning.

METHOD.—Peel the marrow, quarter and seed it. Cut it up into convenient-sized blocks. Boil in enough slightly-salted water to just cover it till tender.

Then lift out and drain the pieces. Put them in a fireproof baking or pie dish. Coat over with cheese sauce, made in the usual way with milk, marrow stock, cornflour, and some of the cheese. Shake over the remaining cheese, and bake till the latter is browned.

Brain Cutlets.—INGREDIENTS.—1 oz. fat, 1 oz. flour, ¾ pint milk, small onion, teaspoon chopped sage, brains, salt, pepper.

METHOD.—Blanch the brains, pick out veins and skins, and chop them. Melt the fat in a saucepan and cook the flour in it for a few minutes, stirring all the time. War-flour needs more cooking than is allowed for in pre-war recipes for white-sauce. Let the sauce cool and add the sage, the onions, chopped up and lightly fried, and and as much chopped brains as will make a stiff mixture. If the quantity is too small, the cutlets may be made partly of brains and partly of boiled rice, which must be well seasoned. Egg-and-bread-crumb and fry in hot fat. The same mixture may be sprinkled with crumbs and baked in a greased fire-proof dish.

Sheeps' Tongues with Savoury Pudding.—INGREDIENTS.—4 sheep's tongues, 1 onion, 1 carrot, 1 turnip, 1 oz. cornflour, 2 tablespoons chopped parsley.

For pudding.—4 oz. flour, 4 oz. cold porridge, 2 oz. sago, 1 tablespoon chopped onion, 1 teaspoon baking powder, 1 teaspoon mixed herbs, salt, pepper.

METHOD.—Well wash and scrape the tongues, the 4 will weigh about 1¼ lb. Lay them in a saucepan with enough cold water to cover them; and a little salt; bring to the boil and skim. Add the vegetables, cleaned and cut in quarters, and let all simmer till the tongues are soft when pierced by a skewer. This should be in about two hours if the pot has been gently simmering the whole time. Peel the tongues and trim them, dish and pour parsley sauce over them. The sauce is made by mixing the cornflour smoothly with a little milk or cold water and stirring it into the boiling stock from which the tongues were taken. Unless the stock is thoroughly stirred while mixing the sauce will be lumpy. Cook gently for a few minutes; add parsley and seasoning.

To make the pudding mix all the ingredients thoroughly, and add water enough to make a soft dough. Steam in a well greased basin for 3 hours, or boil in a pudding cloth for 2 hours. It will save fuel to make the pudding mixture stiff instead of soft, form it into small dumplings and boil them for about half an hour with the tongues.

As The Carmarthen Journal *reported recipes in the local press helped people be creative with limited ingredients.*

On 24th August, 1918, about six months after rationing was introduced, a women's advice column appeared in *The Carmarthen Journal* for the first time. Entitled *"The Woman's Part"* it was written by Margaret Osborne. This weekly column showed housewives how to make food go further, with such delicious sounding recipes as 'vegetable marrow jam', 'brain cutlets', 'sheep's tongues with savoury pudding' and 'marrow á l'indienne'! There were tips on how to make the best of the coal ration and important advice about the Spanish flu (when it struck in 1918). There was a recognition of the importance of healthy women and children for the future of the country, but also an emphasis on the need for women to make way for the men when they returned from the war! The column only appeared for about three months and came to a close with the end of the war. This approach to women's changing role at home and in the community was beginning to be recognised more widely, for example through the advent of the Women's Institute movement. Originating in Canada, the first WI branch in the UK was set up in North Wales in 1915 and grew quickly, though it was several years after the war ended before the WI was established in Laugharne, in 1926.

The demonstration of a motor plough in the county during September, which ploughed twelve acres in a day, was of great interest to local farmers as, at that time, the predominant standard single furrow horse drawn plough was only able to plough one or two acres a day. This onset of mechanised farming would have two benefits over the coming years. The first was to provide a solution to the lack of manpower caused by agricultural labourers joining the forces. Secondly, it had already been recognised that the UK would need to increase food productivity in order to become more self-sufficient due to the difficulties of importing foodstuffs by sea to this island nation. On top of this there was had been a shortage of horses due to them being requisitioned by the army.

During the first week of October a double tragedy struck the Broadway Estate at Laugharne, owned by the South Wales businessman Herbert Eccles. While the workers on the estate were taking in the news that the head gardener's son, Arthur William Cooper, had been killed in France on 3rd October, while serving with the King's Shropshire Light Infantry, the body of the head gamekeeper of the estate was found buried in sand at Laugharne Marsh after he went missing overnight. The gamekeeper, John Garstone, had been hunting for rabbits and he had been digging a burrow in a sand dune when it collapsed on him. The unfortunate man was found with just his feet sticking out from the dune and he was declared dead when he was pulled out. Sadly for Mr Garstone, just a few months previously he had appealed against being conscripted into the army and after an extensive argument he had been exempted until 1st October. If he had enlisted at the time he would have spent the rest of the war in training, and would most likely have survived the conflict!

November, of course, saw the immense news of the signing of the Armistice and the bells of St Martin's, the Town Hall and the School all rang for joy at the news. The newspaper reported that 'general jollification was unbounded' and included a piece on the contribution Laugharne had made (see panel). There was also a Victory Carnival, as the rather blurred photo shows.

> **The Welshman: 15th November, 1918**
> *In the Great War just ended Laugharne has been most patriotic. In proportion to its size and population, it has according to military figures responded second to none in the Kingdom and in the great struggle for freedom and protection Laugharne has also borne its fair share of casualties, in the midst of today's jubilation many here are sad locally, knowing that when neighbours return their dear ones are left behind.*

Laugharne's Victory Carnival.

In the newspaper columns at home there was plenty of good news for local families as the demobilisation of troops began in December and former prisoners of war began to be repatriated. Among these were: Frank Howell, Welsh Regiment, of Causeway; Fred Richards, South Wales Borderers, of Clifton Street; William Isaac, East Yorkshires, of Pendine; and Charlie Lewis, Machine Gun Corps, of Hugdon Cottage. However, this good news was off-set somewhat by news of the influenza epidemic sweeping through the county, with fresh deaths being reported in every town and village almost daily.

While some troops began arriving home, many others had remained in France in order to help the Graves Registration Units and Exhumation Units in identifying and exhuming graves of their comrades, in order to identify them or to concentrate them into cemeteries. Men from Laugharne, who had previously been attached to Labour Companies, continued in these duties for several months.

The Carmarthen War Pensions Committee busied itself resolving the many cases of widowed women and their children, administering money to widows who were still battling the state for their pensions. Headlining the *Laugharne Notes and News* column on 20th December, 1918 was the tale of a young couple holidaying in Pendine. The couple were walking along the beach when they spotted a cask which must have come from a sunken vessel. In an excited state the couple uncorked the cask, each taking a good long swig of the contents. The column went on to state 'Result – medical treatment, which continues at time of writing!'

The same column also carried news of another memorial service at St Martin's Church, a list of men home on leave, and the news of the death of a local serviceman, Private James Richards, who died of cirrhosis. The cessation of hostilities meant the running down of the munitions factory at Pembrey. On Wednesday 11th December the Superintendent of the works, Walter R. Moore, was presented with a large framed photograph of his staff during a well-attended event at the factory. Moore had run the factory for over three years and now returned to his native Scotland. On that same day, two policemen at St Clears apprehended three suspicious looking men, who turned out to be German PoWs who had escaped from Gormwood POW Camp at Llawhaden!

A well-attended fancy dress Victory Ball was held at Laugharne School on Boxing Day. A number of people from the neighbouring towns of Pendine and St Clears made the trip down to celebrate with their neighbours. During the previous week Mrs Turpin, of Temperance House, received a Christmas card which had been posted by her husband from 'Somewhere in France', during December 1914!

Finally, after a couple of years of darkness, David Brown, the Township's lamplighter, took up his duties again – Laugharne's streets were lit once more.

Chapter 3

Laugharne's Fighting Folk

Throughout the war people in Laugharne would be eager for news of what was going on in the war zones, especially where they may have known someone to be involved. That would include a relative, a neighbour, a friend or in reality almost anyone from Laugharne – even from families who had moved away, for they were often still in touch and fondly remembered. So this chapter presents some snippets of the aspects of the war that they would have heard about.

There is already a book, *A Township in Mourning*, which celebrates those men from Laugharne who had fallen and been commemorated on Laugharne's Roll of Honour. However, a book on Laugharne in the Great War would not be complete without some mention of individuals who were involved. So this chapter simply selects a few – those for whom photos or anecdotal recollections exist to illustrate their lives, the hard times they had and sacrifices they all made. It focuses on the war on land – here and in Europe, whilst chapter four will focus on the war at sea.

The chapter concludes with a piece written by a Laugharne soldier, in his own individual style, which expressively presents how he felt about life in the trenches.

WILLIAM CHARLES FULLER

In little more than a month from the start of the Great War Laugharne saw its most famous hero of the conflict, William Charles Fuller, gain the Victoria Cross, Britain's highest award for valour. He was the first Welshman to gain the award in this conflict.

Fuller was born in Newbridge Road, Laugharne, on 13th March, 1884 to William – a sailor and later a butcher – and Mary (nee Fleming), and he had three brothers and four sisters. He was baptised in Laugharne by the Rev. Harrison on May 1st, as the following entry shows:

William Fuller's entry in the baptismal register.

The family had arrived in Carmarthen in 1873 but moved to Laugharne by 1883 and then to Swansea when Fuller was about four, to live at 47 Orchard Street. Educated there at Rutland Street School and then the Swansea Trust School at Bonymaen, William Charles began work as a dock labourer for a few years before enlisting on 31st December, 1902 to serve for seven years in South Africa and India until transferring to the Reserve in 1909. In that same year he married Mary Elizabeth Phillips and took up employment with timber merchants, John Lewis & Sons, and later became the caretaker of the Elysium Cinema in High Street, Swansea. They had five children: Mary Elizabeth (born in 1910), William Charles (born in 1913), Caroline (born in 1916), Doris May (born in 1920) and Muriel (born in 1924).

William C. Fuller, Gazette, 23rd November, 1914.

Following the Declaration of War, Fuller was recalled on 4th August, 1914 and just over a week later he was in France. One month into his war, on 14th September, 1914, near Chivy-sur-Aisne, France, Private Fuller advanced under very heavy enemy rifle and machine-gun fire to extract an officer who was mortally wounded, and carried him back to cover.

Interviewed on 24th November, 1914, about his attempt to save the life of Captain Mark Haggard, he described the event thus:

> On proceeding a little further we were faced by a Maxim gun. There was a little wood on the top and a hedge about 50 yards long. It was not long before the men on Captain Haggard's left were both shot, and

the man on the right was wounded. At the same time Captain Haggard was struck in the stomach, and he fell doubled, the shot coming out through his right side. Thus I was the only one uninjured.

It became necessary for me to carry Captain Haggard back to cover. This was done by him putting his right arm around my neck, while I had my right arm under his legs and the left under his neck. Captain Haggard asked me to lift up his head so that he could see our big guns firing at the Germans as they were retiring from the wood.

Captain Mark Haggard was the nephew of Rider Haggard (the author), and Fuller carried him about 100 yards to a ridge where he stopped to dress the officer's wounds. Captain Haggard asked Private Fuller to fetch his rifle from where he had fallen – he did not want the enemy to get it. So Fuller went back to do that. They waited about an hour there until the firing lessened and they were joined by two other soldiers. With the help of Private Snooks and Lieutenant Melvin, Officer i/c the machine-gun section of the Welsh Regiment, they managed to get Haggard to the safety of a barn that was being used as a First-Aid dressing station.

Private Fuller remained with Captain Haggard until the officer died later on that evening. His last words to Fuller was his battle cry of "Stick it, Welsh." After he died Fuller attended to two other officers (Lt. The Hon Fitzroy Somerset and Lt. Richards) who had also been brought wounded to the barn. The barn then came under heavy fire and the wounded men and officers were evacuated. Later it was razed to the ground by German shell-fire.

Fuller was again mentioned in despatches on 19th October, 1914, and then, while tending a wounded comrade (Private Tagge) near Gheluvelt, Belgium on 29th October, 1914, he was hit by shrapnel in both legs and, as he bent over, a shrapnel ball entered his right side travelled up under the shoulder blade and came to rest against his spine close to his right lung. As a result, Fuller was evacuated to England and treated in Manchester and in Swansea, where a bullet was removed from his neck.

Captain Mark Haggard's widow presented Fuller with a solid gold hunter watch with the bullet taken from Fuller's back moulded into the watch chain and Sir Rider Haggard called on Fuller at his home on 6th January, 1915.

Fuller was gazetted on 23rd November, 1914, and was promoted to Lance Corporal. The news of his award of Victoria Cross was greeted warmly in Laugharne, especially by Mr Tyler as has been seen.

The citation that appeared in the London Gazette of Friday 23rd November, 1914 read:

No. 7753 Lance-Corporal William Fuller, 2nd Battalion, The Welsh Regiment, for conspicuous gallantry on 14th September, near Chivy on the Aisne, by advancing about 100 yards to pick up Captain Haggard, who was mortally wounded and carrying him back to cover under very heavy rifle and machine gun fire.

His Victoria Cross was presented by King George V at Buckingham Palace on 13th January, 1915. Unfit now for further active service, he became a recruiter in Wales, eventually being appointed Acting Corporal in mid-1915 and Sergeant a few months later.

His undoubted bravery was further shown in a different setting: at Fishguard on 19th July, 1915, he was invited to enter the lion's cage of Bostock & Wombwell's Circus. He did so and calmly stroked the animals while chatting to the tamer!

He never forgot his very early links with Laugharne, returning to visit from time to time, as the school log book recorded:

6 March 1918 – Sergeant Fuller, VC, again visited school.

Back home, at first in Evans Terrace then West Cross, Mumbles and later at 55 Westbury Street, Swansea, Fuller ran a horse-drawn fish cart and bred canaries and greyhounds as a hobby, and he also raced the dogs.

William C. Fuller.
[collection of Steve John]

Yet again, on 7th June, 1938 he showed courage by saving two boys from drowning at Tenby slip and was reputedly awarded the Royal Humane Society Medal, though the Society has no record of it.

During the Second World War, Fuller did duty in the Swansea Home Guard as an ARP Warden.

In total, in addition to his Victoria Cross, he received the 1914 Star with Mons clasp, British War Medal 1914-20, Victory Medal 1914-19 with Mentioned in Despatches oak leaf, George VI Coronation Medal of 1937, and Elizabeth II Coronation Medal of 1953. His medals are not publicly held.

Fuller died, aged 90, at his home at 55 Westbury Street, Swansea on 29th December,

1974 and he is buried at Oystermouth Cemetery, The Mumbles, South Wales. For reasons not clear, a headstone was never placed over his grave; the burial plot being marked simply by a small unnamed black vase. A local historian, researching recipients of the Victoria Cross, came across Fuller's unmarked grave and a local newspaper published an article on the find. Several members of the Fuller family came forward and a stone was erected at the grave in 2005.

A commemorative paving stone was also laid in Laugharne in September, 2014, 100 years after his act of bravery.

CHARLES THOMAS LEWIS

Charles Thomas Lewis was born on 17th October, 1895 in Hugdon cottage, the Lacques. He was the youngest of at least seven, possibly up to 10 children, born to John and Esther Lewis (nee Roblin). The siblings, in order of age, were: Frank, Esther, Matilda (Tilly), Alfred (known as Affy), David John, Mary (May), Ann, William and Owen. He was known to his contemporaries as Charley or Chas, but to his family he was just 'Gramps'.

Charley said that his earliest Christmas memory was that of being disappointed when he had asked for a gun, and received a toy pop gun. Of course, what he really wanted was the genuine article. He eventually acquired one and soon became very proficient – his mother would say 'Charley, shoot me a rabbit for dinner', whereupon he would take his gun to the front door and wait for one to appear then take a pot shot – and claimed never to have missed!

Charley as a young man.

At that time Hugdon was a smallholding. The family kept chickens, ducks, geese and turkeys, and possibly pigs. A trout stream ran through the garden from which he taught his grandson to 'tickle' a trout. His first job was as 'Boots' at the Brown's Hotel.

His older sister lived in Llanelli and as a young man, Charley used to cycle the 30 odd miles from Laugharne to visit her. This is where he met Rose Hannah Lewis, and the cycle trips became much more frequent. At the outbreak of war, Charley is said to have travelled all the way to Shrewsbury to join the King's Shropshire Light Infantry (KSLI) since he was anxious to

Rose Hannah.

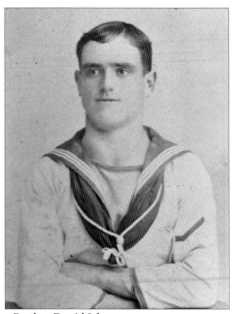

Brother David John was a seaman gunner and saw action at the Battle of Jutland.

HMS St Vincent.
During the battle of Jutland, shells fired from St Vincent hit the light cruiser
SMS Wiesbaden, and later twice made direct hits on the battlecruiser
SMS Moltke before it disappeared into the mist.
Picture Credit: © IWM (Q 21794).

get into action and the KSLI was a regular army regiment of the line and he did not want to wait to join with his pals or brothers. However, at the outbreak of war, the KSLI were on duty in Tipperary and returned via Pembroke Dock where they set up a recruiting office and this is more than likely where Charley enlisted since his first photograph in uniform is stamped on the reverse 'Pembroke Dock'.

His oldest brother, David John, had been in the Navy since 1902, and by the outbreak of war, was a gunner on the dreadnought, HMS St Vincent.

The second oldest brother, Alfred (right), was also already serving – in the Royal Marines Light Infantry. Though two brothers were already in the service, Charley had no interest in trying to team up with either:

> Affy was guarding Pembroke Dock after war broke out, and I wanted to go to Belgium and shoot Germans.

Affy served aboard *HMS Idaho* which was the official name given to the Auxiliary Patrol base at Milford Haven. It took its name from a requisitioned steam yacht – 43 tons (gross) built in 1910. She was taken over by the Navy on 12th April, 1915 and fitted with a heavy machine gun for use as a patrol vessel.

Brother Frank, born on 9th November, 1892, was a Lance Sergeant with the 7th Platoon, B Coy 17th Battalion, King's Liverpool Regiment. This was reputed to be the first of the 'Pals' battalions, although strictly speaking, coming from Laugharne, Frank could not be described as a 'pal'. His battalion, as reported in their war diary, landed in France on 7th November, 1915, but Frank did not see action until the following year, when he joined the battalion as one of the reinforcements after the Battle of Albert in 1916. He would have been involved in battles which took place in close proximity to his brother, Charley, although it seems their paths never crossed.

Frank's battalion was involved in the fighting at St Quentin and Kemmel Ridge in the spring of 1918, when the remnants of his battalion returned to England on 28th June, 1918, Frank probably thought his war was over. However, on 11th October, 1918 he sailed from Glasgow for service in North Russia and remained there until September 1919. His battalion was part of an Allied intervention force assembled to support the 'White forces' in their civil war against the Bolsheviks. The battalion was moved to Archangel.

When Charley went up to Copthorne Barracks, Shrewsbury, for basic training, he was asked if he could shoot, to which he replied by scoring 10 out of 10. He was therefore designated as a 'first class shot'. As he was not quite 19, he was not yet allowed to join the battalion at the front but was offered training as a sniper or a machine gunner. He opted for the latter as it paid an extra 6d a day and it is believed he always sent half his pay back home to his mother.

Charley shared his memories with his family explaining that that they had travelled to London by train, and marched across the city, to leave on another train to Southampton to board a troop ship for France, arriving on 7th July, 1915.

From the outset, Charley would have been issued with a Short Magazine Lee-Enfield (SMLE) Mark III rifle. On average, home leave came around after 14 months service though no notice was given, simply a 'chit' detailing seven days leave, starting immediately. Soldiers would often arrive home filthy, lousy and exhausted. Men going on leave were to carry their rifles to show that they had arrived from the front. The family story has it that he was the first Laugharne man to return on leave from the front and this may have been late 1915. A great deal of fuss was made of the event and his gun, helmet, and boots still caked with Flanders mud were proudly displayed on the Grist for all to see.

The Cross, Grist, Laugharne.

A later picture of Charley after service at the Front.

Charley was proud of his helmet and, at the first opportunity he went to the cook and scrounged several old flour bags to cover his helmet, and those of his Lewis gun section.

Towards the end of 1915, the specialist Machine Gun Corps was formed. Charley was asked if he wished to join, but he declined as he wanted to stay with the battalion and was duly trained as 'A' Company's Lewis gunner.

Charley recalled that the first battle had been involved with was Hooge, which is a small village on the Menin Road (the N8), around two miles east of Ypres. The front line of the Salient was here in 1914 and there was fierce fighting in the area over the next three years, during which the village was totally destroyed. The road from Ypres to Hooge leads past the infamous Hellfire Corner, once one of the most dangerous spots in the Salient. It was a road and rail crossroads, a perfect target for German artillery. A large crater was blown at Hooge on 19th July, 1915. The spoil from the detonation threw up a lip 15 feet high, around a crater, 20 feet deep and 120 feet wide and it was then occupied by British forces. On 30th July, the Germans retaliated with the infamous 'liquid fire' – the first use of flame throwers (Flammenwerfers). The attack involving Charley's 1st KSLI was launched at 3.15am on 9th August. The preceding artillery bombardment was so effective that abandoned flamethrowers were found in the deserted German trenches. Not only was all the lost ground regained and held, in spite of desperate counter-attacks but, in addition, an important spur north of the Menin Road and on the extreme left of the attack, was won and consolidated. The success of this action won great praise for the Division and Lord Plumer, the Army Commander, congratulated the battalion on their success.

After the action, the battalion was relieved by 1st Buffs, and the men returned to dug-outs on the canal bank, before moving into camp between Vlamertinghe and Poperinghe on 11th August. Charley always spoke of Poperinghe ('Pop') with great affection; 'you were safe there, the German guns wouldn't reach that far'.

Charley also saw action on the Somme at Beaumont Hamel, Loos and Cambrai' (pronouncing it 'Cambria' in a Welsh fashion!). He told family that he once '... went to the Estaminet, but I didn't go in' in which he is likely to have meant family to understand that he was a good boy and did not frequent such a place!

The ground around Hooge on the Western Front.

Further research showed that he had been involved in the counter attack on 'Willow Walk' and 'Ducks Bill', German strongholds on the left flank of the 'Estaminet', or to give it its full name: the Morteldje Estaminet.

Benedictine and the lost stripe

At some time between the Second Battle of Ypres and the end of the Battle of the Somme in 1916, Charley 'lost a stripe', meaning he was temporarily demoted. Throughout his life after the war, he had always been against drinking alcohol other than in moderation for medicinal reasons. When asked why, he replied 'I lost a stripe because of it.... but I got it back' (meaning the stripe). As he was a Lewis Gunner, he would have been a corporal or lance corporal with five, and possibly, up to eight 'other ranks' in his section. At some point between times of active duty at the front, he and his section were billeted at a farm. According to the war diary, this would have been during the first few days of April 1916, near Herzeele on the Ypres salient. His section found a farm building to bed down in, and at some point, one of his men found a trap door in the floor which led to a cellar. In the cellar, they found a small keg of Benedictine liqueur. Needless to say, there was none left by morning, and being discovered much the worse for wear by the platoon sergeant, he ended up losing his stripe as punishment. So, Charley's name appeared on the casualty list at the battle of Morval, at the end of the Somme campaign in September 1916, as a private, but his rank at the end of the war was back to Lance Corporal. Being an experienced and trained Lewis gunner, he was an important member of the battalion and soon recovered his rank. Charley also captured a German prisoner (near Loos) which may well also have helped in reinstating his 'stripe'.

Wounded at the Battle of the Somme

Fortunately, Charley was not in action on the infamous first day of the Battle of the Somme. But one month into the battle on 1st August, 1916, his battalion was notified that it would proceed south to join the Reserve Army on the Somme and so on the 15th August, they relieved the Irish Guards' trenches opposite Beaumont-Hamel.

On 14th September, the battalion were part of a force detailed to take the German strong point known as the 'Quad-rilateral', which they achieved after heavy fighting. They then were able to join the main attack on the village of Morval and, in particular, the mill on the ridge north of the village. It was during the attempt to link with the Guards at Les Boeufs, that Charley was wounded in his arm.

Evidence of his stay in Rouen – a bit of 'Trench Art'.

His name appeared on the official casualty lists of the day (published in the Ludlow Advertiser) and he received treatment for his wound in Rouen Military hospital. The wound was not sufficiently serious for him to be sent back to England and so he returned to the battalion. He did however miss the next battle in which the KSLI was involved – the battle of Transloy Ridge, but if he *had* been there, he would have fought alongside his brother Frank, as the 17th King's Liverpool Regiment also took part in this battle. This was one of the last battles of the Somme campaign.

The Mirror story

The mirror, leaning on another souvenir: a German Stahlhelm helmet.

Charley's daughter had always told her son that he should not ask his grandfather about the war as it was too painful for him to talk about as all his pals were 'blown to bits' when he was wounded and taken prisoner. It was not until the late 60s or 70s that he started talking about his experiences and the battles he fought in.

In the family kitchen (the 'scullery') a battered old mirror hung on the wall near the sink which Charley used when shaving. When asked why such a battered old thing was kept and where it had come from, Charley replied 'Loos'. He recounted the story: following the Allies bombardment of the German lines, he was in one of the patrols sent out, and as a Lewis gunner, he would be supporting the first wave sent to infiltrate the trenches, consolidate any captured positions and deal with any enemy counter-attack.

Together with his section he entered the enemy lines and on reaching the main forward trench found a solitary German, sitting with his back to the parapet holding a mirror up above the top to see any movement from the British lines. Charley cocked his revolver, pointed it at the German and said: "Hands up Fritz", to which he replied: "Don't shoot me Tommy. Here take this mirror. It will be more use to you now than to me". Charley did not shoot him, but took him back as his prisoner to their own trenches. There Charley had a chance to ask him how he spoke such good English, and the German explained that he had worked as a waiter in a hotel in Liverpool before the War!

The mirror remained one of Charley's 'spoils of war' and he most probably brought it back home to Wales when on leave, or kept it safely in his 'valise' held in the reserve trenches when he was in the front line.

Battle of Cambrai, Marcoing and the Gas Cape

On Charley's 22nd birthday, 17th October, 1917, his battalion was ordered to join the 6th Division which was resting prior to joining 3rd Army for Battle of Cambrai. They reached Ivenrgny by October 30th where they spent some

Railway Bridge at Marcoing over the canal, partially
destroyed prior to 3rd December 1917.
[Imperial War Museum (Q45412)]

time practising attacks with tanks. The battalion then proceeded by train to
Peronne and marched northwards from there. As a Lewis gunner, Charley would
sometimes travel by cart, or some other form of transport, though usually the
'PBI' (Poor Bloody Infantry) would get from A to B on foot. 'Infantry, after all,
were foot soldiers', he would say.

The battalion left camp at d'Essart Woods, and took up its position for the
attack on Hindenburg Line, south of Cambrai, which was their first objective.

After much to-ing and fro-ing, his battalion found themselves, by the end
of November, on the east side of the St Quentin Canal where they were subject
to shell, rifle and machine gun fire from the north, south and east. Following
wave after wave of attack and counter-attack, according to the battalion and
brigade war diaries:

> After fighting a desperate but gallant rear-guard action, the battalion
> managed to extricate itself, with many officers and men having to swim
> the canal to safety.

As a postscript to Charley's experiences at the canal, he once explained to his
grandson how he had wrapped his Lewis gun in his gas cape, and he and his
section then lashed it and their ammunition drums (covered in groundsheets)
to some planks of wood from a nearby destroyed bridge. They were then able
to push it and drag it across a 'river' (as he described the canal) to safety.

Spring 1918: Charley's role in the last big German offensive

Charley's battalion's war diary reports a growing sense of foreboding around the unusual amount of enemy activity and the men were constantly ordered to 'stand to' at battle positions from 4am – 8am. The enemy's intentions were clear.

The German offensive began just before 5am on the 21st March with an intense bombardment which lasted for 5 hours. Half of the entire German artillery in the west was amassed along a 50 mile front. 6,500 artillery pieces, firing over a million shells together with 3,500 mortars were used against the British lines. The enemy attacked with Storm Trooper infantry equipped with the latest equipment: flame throwers, hand grenades and light machine guns. The attack was launched with great dash and overwhelming superiority of numbers, many troops having been released from the Eastern Front. Charley and his fellow KSLI soldiers were overrun by German forces. A and B companies were almost annihilated in the first hour and a half of the bombardment, and by 7am the enemy was reported to be through. The officer who completed the entry in the 1st Battalion, KSLI war diary for the 22nd March wrote:

> In this the heaviest fighting the battalion has ever known, i.e. 21-22nd March 1918, the Battalion loss was: killed, wounded, & missing, 21 officers and 492 other ranks, and despite the heavy losses, it earned for itself the admiration of all who fought and added fresh laurels to the history of a gallant Regiment.

Only 77 'other ranks' survived on the evening of 22nd March.

This was one event that Charley would not talk about but research shows that his post was hit by a gas shell during the bombardment. All of his section (probably seven men) were killed outright. The Germans were using heavy ordnance (four parts gas, one part high explosive) and the gas used was Green Cross Phosgene. Charley was wounded in the leg by a fragment from the gas shell casing. By some sort of miracle, he was 'swept up' by the advancing Germans and taken back to a German casualty or dressing station.

The Germans had organised their rail system to link the front line with their cities in Germany, which meant Charley was put on a train and found himself in a military hospital in Berlin. As a result of the poison, Charley's leg 'swelled to twice its size', and at some point a junior doctor was planning to amputate but, fortunately, a senior surgeon saw the wound and said that there was no

Lfd. Nr.	a) Familienname b) Vorname (nur der Rufname) c) nur bei Russen Vorname des Vaters	Dienst-grad	a) Truppen-teil b) c) Komp.	a) Gefangennahme (Ort und Tag) b) c) vorhergehender Auf-enthaltsort	a) Geburtstag und Ort b) Adresse des nächsten c) Verwandten
21.	a) LIVERPET b) John c) 74324	Gem.	15th. York & Lincs. C K16	a) Irvillers.25/3/18 b) Nicht Verw. c) West Front	a) 26.11.88.London. b) London. c)
22.	a) LARSON b) Arthur c) 125	Gem.	18th. W.Yorks. C K16	a) Ervillers.27/3/18 b) Nicht Verw. c) West Front	a) 24.9.81.Yeadon. b) Windermere. c) - do -
23.	a) LEE b) Herbert c) 57804	Gem.	2/6th. Sherwood Foresters. K16	a) Socoust.21/3/18 b) Nicht Verw. c) West Front	a) 27.9.93.Leeds. b) Nottingham. c) - do -
24.	a) LEWIS b) Charles c) 16035	L/Cpl.	1st. K.S.L.I. A K16	a) Lagnicourt.21/3/18 b) Nicht Verw. c) West Front	a) 17.11.96.Langharne. b) Langharne. c) - do -
25.	a) LEARMOUTH b) Arthur c) 267784	L/Cpl.	1/6th. Black-Watch. B K16	a) Pronville.21/3/18 b) Nicht Verw. c) West Front	a) 2.12.81.Isaazeen. b) Balmullo. c) - do -
26.	a) LEES b) Leonard c)	Gem.	1st. W.Yorks. D K16	a) Pronville.21/3/18 b) Nicht Verw. c) West Front	a) 28.8.93.Oldham. b) Oldham. c) - do -

The POW registration document, supplied by the Red Cross

"Sorry Klara, I have a sweetheart back home in Wales. Here, see my locket".

need to amputate. He had recognised the symptoms of gas poisoning and that it could be treated effectively; Charley's leg was saved. Whilst in hospital he was be-friended by a nurse, Klara, from Saxony. Charley told family that she had asked if he would marry her and take her back to 'England' after the war. He, of course, declined saying that he already had a sweetheart back home.

Following recovery, Charley was shipped off to Parchim, a prisoner of war camp in the Mecklenburg area of north Germany.

Charley was able to describe in detail the story of his capture. By 11.00 am over three quarters of the battalion were killed, wounded or taken prisoner, though he never spoke much about this aspect of the experience, just that he had been wounded and picked up by the Germans.

Meanwhile, back home, the message had been received that he was 'missing in action' on 21st or 22nd March. All too frequently this meant 'probably dead'. But Rose Hannah, his sweetheart, pressed for more information. Months went by with no news. She even resorted to visiting a clairvoyant who told her that the one she was waiting for was still alive and to wait for his return. This was eventually confirmed in June, but still she pressed on, to receive another only slightly more helpful letter in August from a Lieutenant Bunker, referring her to contact Sergeant Whitney. Sergeant Whitney had been one of just four captured KSLI men who eventually managed to escape back to the British lines.

Charley's POW camp had been built early in the war to house 25,000 prisoners from the Eastern Front. However, by the time Charley arrived, the number had risen to 45,000 prisoners! During his confinement, he

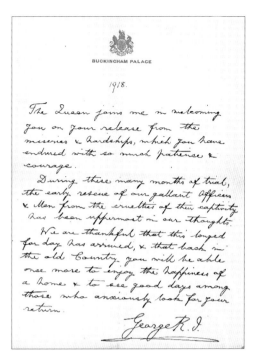

learned some essential phrases of German – 'Kriegsgefangenenlager, Parchim Mecklenburg', which was effectively his address and knowing it ensured he would not get shot if he was challenged while working in the fields outside the camp! His other German phrase was: 'geh raus Tommy' which was what the German guards would shout while banging on the hut door in the morning. He hated being a POW. 'We were jam packed', he said, and he claimed the worst thing about the experience was the food, or lack of it – 'The bread was black!'

Between the Armistice in November 1918 and mid-January 1919, British POWs held in north Germany were repatriated via Denmark and the Baltic ports in an operation known as the 'Danish Scheme'. Charley said that his ship left Danzig, and they sailed through the Skagerrak and Kattegat straits heavily mined by the Germans, with two Danish sharpshooters on the bows of the ship, popping off the mines one by one to the cheers of the Tommies on board. The ship docked at Hull and soon after a check-up at the army camp at Ripon for liberated POWs, he returned to his beloved Wales – to the joy and relief of his whole family. As a returning POW he received a letter of empathy from the King. Charley was eventually discharged on 19th March, 1919, and following his return home, he married his fiancée, Rose Hannah. They had one child, a daughter born in December 1921.

During the Second World War, Charley worked in a steel foundry making bomb casings as well as mysterious looking cast iron components, which turned out to be sections of the Mulberry Harbour bridge used on D-Day. A rather officious manager (a Captain Mainwaring type) tried to set up a Home Guard unit at the foundry, and wanted Charley, as an old soldier, to drill with the men carrying pick axe handles. Charley refused and said: 'I'm not doing any more square-bashing, just give me a Lewis gun and I will go on the roof and shoot down any German plane that comes near'.

The final piece of Charley's story is that he always said that his mother lived until she was 86 and he was determined to live to that age, too. He died of pneumonia in Llanelli hospital, at the age of 86, on Christmas day 1981.

BILLY HARRY AND ELEANOR WATTS (as told to a local resident)

BILLY HARRY

Billy Harry retired to live opposite our house in Holloway Road in the 1950s. He would tell my father about his wartime experiences working in the Pembrey munitions factory. As children we would very often be listening. Billy was quite a humorous person.

Whilst working at the munitions factory he stayed in lodgings in nearby Llanelli. One tale he told us was about his first landlady who had a number of lodgers, all working in the munitions factory during the war.

At first they had satisfactory meals but as time went by the meals became very much smaller. One morning he asked her who had buttered his bread. She answered him quite sharply, 'I did'. He then asked her quite seriously, 'Well who the hell took it off my bread!?' The other lodgers all agreed. The meals then improved, but he soon found another and better place to lodge!

He told us that the Pembrey Munitions factory had been built mainly on sand hills and sand dunes. This provided protection against damage caused by any explosion. It was also quite remote. In the war women from all parts of society took on jobs previously undertaken by men who had all joined the forces. Most importantly these women reported for work at the munitions factory in droves. He told us that it was difficult and dangerous work. The munitions workers, mostly women, gave many reasons for working in these factories. Many of them told him that it was 'patriotism' – helping their country – as most of them had relatives fighting in the war: fathers, brothers, uncles, etc. Mostly, however, it was for the wages. They were advertising for munitions workers with good money. On average many women had been earning only about five shillings (25p) per week in domestic service. They could now earn up to £3 with overtime, in munitions. Most earned about £2 to £2.50 which was considered to be a small fortune by many women at that time! Even so, Billy told us that female workers received less pay than their male workmates.

They were, however, very frank in saying that their main reason for working in TNT (munitions) was for the money as, before the war there were few jobs for women, except as domestic servants. He said that many told him they had been in service, where they worked hard and did their best. Their 'mistresses' had criticised them and had been very sarcastic, never thanking them, even when doing extra work. The women workers told him it was a big feeling of relief to leave those sarcastic 'mistresses' and have a job in the munitions factory.

Billy said that in the factory they were constantly under surveillance for safety and always reminded of the dangers. It was emphasised to all of them that no tobacco or metal objects, e.g. knives, were allowed to be taken into the munitions factory. He also said that when an explosion occurred in a munition works in another part of the country they would be told about it, to emphasise the dangers of the jobs they were carrying out. However, they would never, or very rarely, be published in the newspapers since it was top secret work.

In every factory there was a 'danger zone' where the work of filling shells with TNT was carried out. The finished shells were stored in the munitions shed in lines on the floor. The women worked in four hour shifts and were utterly exhausted at the end of their shift. They had meal breaks for an hour for which they brought in their own sandwiches and pies.

Working with TNT meant they could turn yellow as a result of being in contact with the powdered explosives. Masks and overalls helped stop this eventually. They were also each given a pint of cold milk to neutralise the effects of the poisonous explosives they handled.

The female munitions workers would often put notes into the cases of the shells, wishing the soldiers good luck. As they told him, they wanted to cheer them up. Billy told us about the soldier who found one of the notes from a munitions worker. He wrote to her asking her for a date when he came home on leave. He came home on leave and took her out. The great surprise was that they got married by special licence after only four days together!

Billy Harry always said that the real dangers came from accidents. Despite all the precautions and warnings, accidents sometimes took place. Sometimes a bullet would explode and workers might lose fingers or even worse. He told us that all the munitions workers admired the doctors and nurses who worked extremely hard with their customary devotion to duty, particularly when there was an accident in the munitions factories. One of the victims of such an accident was my Aunt Nellie.

ELEANOR "NELLIE" WATTS

Eleanor Watts, 'Nellie' as she was called, was born in Lower Gosport Street, Laugharne in 1891, and actually christened Mary Ellen Watts. She was known to us as 'Aunt Nellie', and was the eldest of seven children born to Elizabeth and John Watts.

Elizabeth Watts, formerly Brigstocke, worked in Strand House in domestic service. John Watts worked in Brixtarw Farm, Laugharne. They were married in 1891 but, like many others at the time, John Watts went to work as a collier in Cwmparc, near Treorchy, Rhondda Valley – for better pay! They would return home at weekends – by train to Ferryside then walk across to the Laugharne ferry bell-house to call for the ferry to bring them over to Laugharne. Elizabeth brought all their children up in Lower Gosport Street. Elizabeth Watts, known locally as 'Mam' Watts, was very popular in the area, and well known for her kindness. To my sister and me she was 'Granny' Watts.

In 1911, aged 20, like many others, Nellie moved away to look for work in a town. She found a job in a shop in Swansea, and shortly after moving there she met her husband, Bert Bibby. They had three children – Haydn, May and Bertie.

Nellie's husband, Bert, was called up to serve in the war in 1916 and, along with thousands of other soldiers, he was killed at the Battle of the Somme. This left Nellie as a widow with three small children and she found life very difficult, as there was very little family benefit at this time. She therefore had to find a job. This she found in the Munitions Factory in Pembrey and while she worked, her children were looked after by her in-laws.

The munitions factory was a very dangerous place to work. Accidents often occurred and the workers had constant warnings of the dangers. In 1917 an accident occurred in the 'danger zone' of the Pembrey works. There was a relatively small explosion but some of the women involved were seriously injured and Nellie was one of them.

Nellie suffered terrible injuries: she lost one eye, had a broken nose and her face was badly mutilated. This small group of workers had done everything

Removing plugs from time fuses.
[Source: National Archives]

Removing 18Pdr shells from cartridge case.
[Source: National Archives]

correctly in their particular tasks and the explosion was entirely unexpected. A bullet had exploded and set off the explosion – the women were extremely lucky not to have been killed.

Nellie belonged to a union which obtained compensation for the women from this accident and with the compensation Nellie was able to buy a house in Sketty, Swansea. But life was still difficult for her as she needed money to look after the newly purchased house, as well as bringing up her three small children. So she invited two of her sisters from Laugharne to lodge with her, and they found jobs in shops, which suited them well. They were our Aunty Con and Aunty Peg. A short time later, in 1918, one of the sisters married. Peace had now been declared, Germany had been defeated, and the soldiers were being demobbed in their thousands, including her brother, Ben Watts, our Uncle Ben.

Ben and his younger brother, Johnny Watts, my father, had failed to find steady jobs in Laugharne, so Nellie invited them to lodge with her in Sketty as there were some jobs going in Swansea. The brothers found jobs with a transport company, and, of course, this was a great help to Nellie during this difficult time after the war. The brothers lodged with Nellie until 1931 when they moved back to Laugharne. Ben went back to building and eventually joined the 'Pendine Establishment'. Johnny became an Insurance Agent and eventually Laugharne's postman.

Nellie's wartime experience left her scarred for life. She always refused to be in any family photograph so, sadly, we cannot include one of her here.

WILLIAM JENKINS

William Jenkins' birth certificate.

William Jenkins was born to parents Joshua (19, a labourer) and Sarah (31, nee James) at Hare's Head in the Parish of Laugharne on June 3rd, 1875. The family moved to Llanddowror so he was educated at Llanddowror Church School. On leaving school he worked as a farm servant at Well Stone, Eglwys Cymin, and then as a timber feller. He married Catherine and by 1901 they had a daughter and lived at Brick House Cottage near Brixtarw. Ten years later, like many others, he had become a miner and the couple had moved to Porthcawl with their 6 children: Katie (then aged 13), Sarah (12), Martha (10), James J. (4), Margery M (3) and William J (1).

100

William Jenkins.

On June 27th, 1915 he joined the Glamorganshire Yeomanry as Private, Regimental Number 2304. On October 12th, 1916 he was transferred to the 24th Welsh regiment, Number 320915 and again in December 1918 to the Labour Battalion.

He served on the Western Front and in Egypt from March 1916 until October 1916, and from October 1916 to March 1918 he served with the 24th Welsh on the Palestinian Front, 74 Yeomanry Division. He was present at the Battle of Beersheba and other engagements in Palestine. He suffered from Malaria in Egypt and was for a time at the Cairo Hospital. From the 1st May, 1918 until Christmas the same year he served with the Labour Battalion in France. He was demobilised in December 1918, Category B.II, evidently having suffered from his experience in the war.

He is commemorated in the Llanddowror Book of Remembrance.

THOMAS JOHN HARRY

Thomas Harry was born in 1883 and by 1911 was married, to Ellen, and they had three young children: Llewellyn (aged 4 in 1911), Lillian (2) and Frederick (2 months). He was working as a mason labourer and they lived in a 4-roomed house in Horsepool Road, Laugharne.

He enlisted on 8th December, 1915 with the Royal Field Artillary Territorial Force, and joined the 1st Brigade East Lancs Division (Number 701521) 2nd Reserve Brigade at Bettisfield Park. He was discharged on 5th November, 1918, with wounds. A photo shows the injured soldier, wearing a blue armband, and clearly the wound to his leg continued to trouble him, since *The Narberth Weekly News* 12th March, 1925 reported:

> Admitted to hospital – Mr Thomas Harry, Clifton Street, was admitted to Chepstow Military Hospital for the purpose of having his leg (which was severely wounded in the war) operated upon – we hope it is a success.

Thomas Harry, as marked X.

Tom Harry, wearing his wound armband.

Although clearly damaged for life by the war, the operation presumably worked to some extent because he helped with the building of Laugharne's Memorial Hall, which opened in March, 1926.

The couple gave birth to twins in 1921 and Thomas found work with horses at East Hill Farm. He lived to the age of 64, by which time he had moved to 1, Church Street.

WILLIAM CONSTABLE

The Prologue mentioned young William Constable in his pre-war situation when he was a boy scout and worked as an assistant in a men's outfitters. He was just one of many local young men who served in World War 1, but it is fortunate that more information about him is still available compared to many of the others. He was born in 1898, the middle child of five living with their mother, Jane, and grandmother, Bridget, in a large house in Horsepool Road. His father, Philip, was an engineer on chartered sea vessels and even wore his sea uniform whilst home, seemingly anxious to get back to sea again!

In 1915 William enlisted, in Finsbury, into the Royal Welsh Fusiliers, whose contingent entered the war on the 5th December, 1915. This photograph shows them relaxing outside their billets, William indicated by the X, a few weeks before departure.

William Constable with his fellow soldiers.

Although records list him as a Private, at some point William seems to have been promoted to Corporal, as the next photo shows a stripe on each arm. A number of men from the 38th (Welsh) Division became attached to the 255th Tunnelling Company during their early months at the front, working in the

Cambrin and Cuinchy sectors. William was among them. Their job, fraught with danger, was to dig tunnels under no-man's land to reach the enemy lines and plant them with explosives. After the battles of the Somme they were moved to Ypres to blow mines at Messines and Hooge.

Having successfully survived 1916, William and his battalion were moved back behind the front lines at Trois Tours for further training and relaxation before return to the front. This supposedly 'safe' position proved otherwise when, on 28th January 1917, a shell from German long range guns landed on his billets, killing him and his comrades. He was not yet 19 years old.

For his part in the war offensive William was awarded the 1914/15 Star; the British War Medal, and the Victory Medal.

His death was not recorded in the local newspapers – was this policy or negligence? The effect of his death on his family is not known, but it would have been compounded by their fears for his two brothers, Neville and John, who had also enlisted. Fortunately they survived the war physically unharmed.

William Constable wearing his Corporal's stripe.

BEN WATTS

Ben Watts' lucky escape

Benjamin Watts was the second eldest of seven children born to Elizabeth ('Mam') and John Watts in Lower Gosport Street. Born in 1898, he was too young to enter service in the early years of the First World War. But so many men had been killed in the war that in January 1916 a Military Service Act was passed conscripting all men between the ages of 18 and 41. So 18 year old Ben was called up.

He travelled by horse and trap to St Clears Station and on by train to the recruiting camp at Brecon, before being sent on to North Wales for eight weeks of military training. During a week's leave he told his family about life in the army and predicted he would be sent to France, where of course the chances were high that he would also be killed.

Shortly after his leave, however, his Mam learned that instead he had been sent by troop ship to Mesopotamia (now Iraq), to capture the oilfields there from the Turks. In Mesopotamia the greatest dangers turned out not to be from fighting but from diseases such as dysentry, cholera and malaria and from the heat, which Ben claimed to be worse than the enemy!

In February 1917, in the second battle of Kut, the British army overwhelmed the Turks and captured Baghdad under their Commander, General Maude. Later that year they captured Tikrit and the oilfields there. By autumn 1918 they had also captured the oil town of Mosul and the Turkish army surrendered. So for a short while Ben became a Prisoner of War camp guard.

However, soon after the surrender came through the troops there learned to their great consternation that they were now to be posted to the war front in Europe. That was certainly unwelcome news. However, within just a few hours of that shock came further news that in fact the war had ended just the day before! Not only had they escaped the transfer to deadly warfare in Europe, but they were to return to 'Blighty'. Once there most, including Ben, were demobbed.

On arriving home most soldiers were treated for a short while as heroes. However, then reality set in. Ben wanted to go back to his work as a builder but there was no work to be had in Laugharne, so together with his brother Johnny he moved to Swansea, to lodge with their sister and he got work with a transport firm.

ERIC WESTERN WILSON

In September, 1914 the British Expeditionary Force suffered terrible casualties at the Aisne, amongst them one from Laugharne – the first from the Township to fall – Eric Western Wilson, aged just 21.

He had been born in 1893 at Thornton-le-Moor, Yorkshire, the only son of John Western Wilson and Caroline Mary Wilson. The family moved to The Cors, Laugharne when Eric was young, and he was educated at Carmarthen Grammar School, Kelly College and Leeds University. Commissioned as a second lieutenant into the Special Reserve, the Prince of Wales' Own West

Eric Western Wilson.

Yorkshire Regiment, in July 1913, he was posted to their 1st Battalion at the outbreak of war.

On 20th September, 1914, he was leading his platoon to recapture a trench near Troyon, France, which had been lost earlier in the day, and he was shot by German machine-gun fire. He has no known grave and is remembered on the La Ferté-sous-Jouarre Memorial.

In October his widowed mother, Caroline Mary Wilson, received a telegram informing her of her son's death:

> Buckingham Palace, Oct. 4th, 1914. The King and Queen deeply regret the loss you and the Army have sustained by the loss of your son in the service of their country. Their Majesties truly sympathise with you in your great sorrow.

It was rapidly followed by a letter from his Sergeant, J.T. Woodcock:

> At the Battle of the Aisne, on the fatal day, Sept. 20th, the West Yorks were called to advance 200 yards to small trenches, the range of which the Germans had exactly, and they were mown down like sheep. At six o'clock they ran out of ammunition and the Germans made up their minds to charge. Our captains gave orders to fix bayonets, but the Germans first charged their magazines and then rushed at us, and fired when about ten yards away…

Woodcock was himself also shot and wounded in the attack, but was one of just 206 survivors of the battalion, from a strength of almost 1,200.

Another man, from a different battalion involved in the action, wrote of what he had seen:

> On September 20th, the Germans somehow or other got to the back of our trenches. They came down in column formation, and were flying the white flag. As soon as our fellows went up to take them as prisoners the first row opened fire on the West Yorks. Our regiment then went up with fixed bayonets and drove them out of the trenches. We lost a good number of men killed and wounded in that charge.

News of such outrages, as well as others that were made up (what would now be called *fake news*) was publicised widely in the press to help bolster recruitment, but it cannot have been of much comfort to the bereaved.

George William Brown was born in Laugharne on 26th July, 1885, the son of Harry and Sarah Brown, of the Grist. He had enlisted into the Royal Navy on 22nd December, 1903 and trained as a Stoker at *HMS Vivid* before being posted aboard *HMS Challenger* on 31st May, 1904. On 3rd August, 1904 he transferred to *HMS Euralyus*, spending almost two years aboard before returning to *HMS Vivid*.

Then, in January 1907, George was posted aboard *HMS Hibernia*, but got himself into trouble with the authorities on several occasions, which saw him being awarded three separate spells of incarceration. He was discharged from the Royal Navy on 2nd January, 1909, deemed as unsuitable for transferring to the Royal Naval Reserve due to his character, despite his papers showing that he was very proficient in his work.

Following the outbreak of war George volunteered for the Royal Field Artillery and was posted to France.

During December 1915 he was lucky to escape with his life after being badly wounded by machine-gun fire, suffering bullet wounds to his chest, just missing

Royal Field Artillery gun.

his heart and coming out through his loin. He also suffered wounds to his left arm, leg and feet. Badly wounded, George was slowly brought back to England via the chain of casualty clearing stations and spent several months in hospital at Lincoln.

Sergeant George Brown was finally released from Lincoln Hospital during June 1916 and returned home to his parents in Laugharne. However, he was left disillusioned with his return, as he was not afforded the welcome he felt he deserved. A report from the local correspondent in *The Welshman* stated:

> Tuesday last was his first visit home since joining H.M. Forces, and out-side his immediate family the reception given to him in his native town was anything but British. Instead of being given the reception a much battered and suffering hero should have had, no one seems to have enquired whether he had anything to eat or drink. This is not the first native that has come home wounded to Laugharne and been given the cold shoulder. Strangers are given every welcome and hospitality is heaped upon them. No expense is spared to lavish upon able-bodied Belgians, whereas when a wounded native arrives, no one enquires whether he has place to lay his head down. Sergeant Brown left Laugharne on Friday "fed-up", as he put it, with his native town…

Part of his upset may have been because Able Seaman Aubrey Graham Edwards, on leave from the Royal Naval Reserve at the same time that George was home, was given a much better welcome, being invited to attend a specially arranged Big Court to be sworn in as a Burgess. He had not even been on active service at that point!

Little else is known of George, but his younger brother John, born on 8th October, 1895, served with the Royal Navy during the war and lived until 1949.

A satirical postcard referring to the Kaiser's description of the British Army.

Those engaged in the war frequently sent home letters and cards, such as this one, posted from *HMS Hampshire* in 1915, which depicts the astonishing involvement of troops from numerous countries all over the world in support of the Allies. Many of those troops included men from families, or individuals like David Thomas John, who had emigrated from Britain, from Laugharne – as the following examples illustrate.

DAVID THOMAS JOHN
AND HIS BROTHER, JAMES JOHN

David Thomas John was born in Llanelli in 1891, although his brother John was born in Tylorstown, Glamorgan, four years later, where his father was then employed as a coalminer. But then the family moved to Halfpenny Furze, Laugharne, and both boys went to Llanddowror School. Sadly his mother, Eliza John, was widowed in 1903 when her husband William drowned while bathing at Pendine.

David Thomas John.

Two months after his own son was born David John ran away from his family in Halfpenny Furze to begin a new life in Australia, leaving his wife and young son behind. Within less than a year the Great War broke out and on the 8th August he became the first Laugharne man to enlist, signing up at Randwick into the 4th Battalion, Australian Imperial Force.

Having survived the tragic Gallipoli campaign his battalion sailed aboard the troopship *Transylvania* for Marseilles and then moved to Flanders. The Battle of the Somme had been launched at 6.20am on 1st July, 1916 but the first attacks failed to make any real gains so the Australians were summoned. David's battalion attacked Pozières alongside the 8th Battalion on 23rd July and took part in some of the most brutal and gruesome fighting that the Australians had seen since the previous year. Within two days Pozières was taken and over the coming days the front line pushed forward, inch by bloody inch.

Unlike hundreds of his comrades David survived the Battle of Pozières, and was among the shell-shocked, battle-weary troops who marched through Albert back to their rest area at Warloy-Baillon.

By 17th August, his battalion had moved forward again, and on the morning of 18th August it was warned to prepare for an assault on the heavily fortified Mouquet Farm that afternoon. David was ordered out to reconnoitre the area in front of the Australian trenches. At 2.00pm he led his three comrades off, sneaking over the parapet to crawl across No Man's Land, in broad daylight, towards the German outpost defences. They crept through the barbed wire and made their way into the German trenches safely, but were then surprised by a German patrol which came around the corner of the trench. They managed to escape but then became trapped and attacked by bombers, replying to their fire with some of their own grenades. Two men returned safely to their own lines, but not David and Private Oliver Williams. They had been killed – their bodies never recovered.

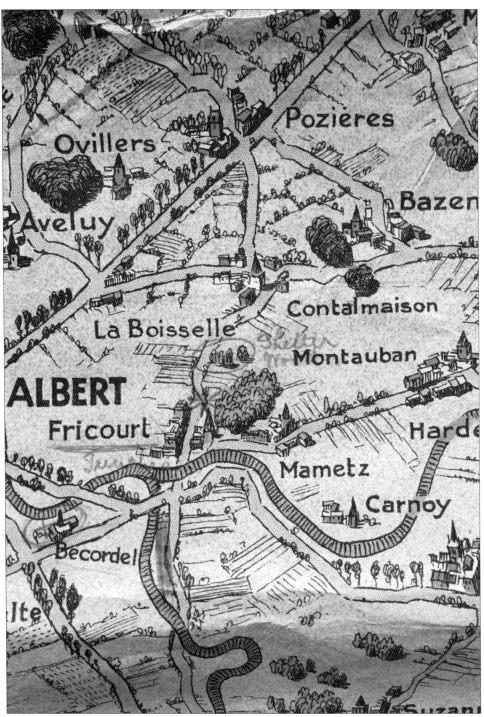

Part of a Daily Mail map sold for people at home to be able to follow the accounts of war.
It bears pencil markings around Fricourt where someone has done just that.

Mouquet Farm quarry.

Like thousands of others killed on the Somme, he has no known grave but is commemorated on the Villers-Brettoneux Memorial and in the Llanddowror Book of Remembrance. Relatives back in Laugharne, as throughout the country, would not have been able to express their grief through the ritual of a funeral.

David's younger brother, John, joined the Pembrokeshire Yeomanry in May, 1915, aged 20, and served with them through 1916 and 1917 in Egypt, suffering great hardships on the march to Palestine where he took part in engagements at Gaza and Beersheba. In May, 1918, like his brother had been before him, he too was then transferred to France with the 24th Welsh for an advance on the Somme.

On 21st September, 1918, the 74th (Yeomanry) Division was thrown into action at Épehy, to capture the German stronghold at Gillemont Farm. There, the 24th Welsh got bogged down and suffered heavy casualties. Some 10 county men were killed in the attack on the farm, six of whom were 24th Welsh men. Four of these men were from the original Pembroke Yeomanry contingent who had arrived in Egypt in 1916, including Private John James John. He is buried at Unicorn British Cemetery and commemorated in the Llanddowror Book of Remembrance.

William Neville with his wife, Hannah.

In chapter two Mrs Minnie Peel is described as 'The Angel of Laugharne' for all the good work she did, especially for the war effort. Her husband had died leaving her with four children to raise – three boys and one girl, Dulcie, who also contributed to the war effort herself.

Francis, the eldest, went to South Africa and fought in the Boer Wars and he served with the Brabant's Horse. He died in 1918 when working as an engineer in the mines. Ralph, also confusingly known as Billy, went to Canada and farmed. William was known as Neville and at the age of 17 he joined Francis in South Africa before going to Canada. At some point he reputedly ran off with a circus girl! In Canada he joined the 8th Battalion Canadian Infantry.

Having joined the Canadian Expeditionary Force (CEF), he embarked on the troop ship *SS Empress of Britain* and arrived in England on 11th November, 1916, spending a short spell at Laugharne on leave, before being transferred to the 8th (Manitoba) Battalion. As part of the Battle of Arras, the Canadian Corps made its famous assault on Vimy Ridge on 9th April, capturing the German positions which had dominated the area since the early days of the war. His battalion was in reserve during the capture of Vimy Ridge, but played a full part in further operations, mopping up German positions to the east of the ridge. On 25th April the battalion was sent forward with orders given to attack the village of Arleux-En-Gohelle, which was taken on the next day. But the battalion's war diary states that resistance was stubborn, with hand-to-hand fighting taking place in the village. Peel was killed in action on 28th April, 1917 and was buried in Orchard Dump Cemetery.

It is often thought that 'going over the top' was the greatest horror of the war, as of course it was. But everyday trench life was also horrendous much of the time. To raise one's head was to risk a bullet in it. Constant rain led to severe cases of 'trench-foot'. For lengthy spells there was also the boredom. Many servicemen wrote journals or poems to help them bear it all, Merlin was one of them.

He was born on 16th April, 1896 to Esther Watts, a farm servant from Llansadwrnen. His mother married David Price, of Sarland Farm in 1904 and Merlin worked on that farm in the coming years. In the summer of 1916 Merlin received his call-up papers, but his step-father appealed against his most valuable worker going off to war and an exemption was granted on a temporary basis until another worker could be found to replace him.

Later in 1916 Merlin enlisted into the Monmouthshire Regiment. He spent the early months of 1917 training at Brecon but was taken seriously ill in March 1917, spending some time in hospital. He married Margaret Anne Evans whilst on leave soon afterwards.

Merlin Watts.

After fully recovering from his illness Merlin was posted to France and was transferred to the 12th Battalion, Gloucestershire Regiment, known as 'Bristol's Own' and attached to 95 Brigade, 5th Division. The division had been recalled from Italy to France following the German offensive of 21st March, 1918. Several weeks of terrible fighting followed before the fighting moved southwards, when the Germans launched their third, last ditch, offensive in the Champagne sector in May 1918.

By this time Merlin's battalion had settled down in a sector north of the town of Merville, by the village of Caudescure. At 6.00am on 28th June, 1918 the battalion took part in a combined attack against several German defensive positions facing the village.

Merlin arose alongside his comrades from their front-line trench and followed a rolling barrage across the battlefield before entering the German positions facing them. Despite heavy machine-gun fire the assault proved successful, with all of the objectives being taken and consolidated.

For his gallantry during the assault, Merlin was awarded the Military Medal, an award selected for men who had shown 'Bravery in the Field', and his citation, 'for conspicuous gallantry and devotion to duty in action' was signed by Lieutenant General Richard Haking, commander of XI Corps. It was published in the London Gazette of 13th November, 1918.

Merlin survived the war and returned home to Sarland Farm where he settled down with Margaret, before taking over the farm at Roger's Well. He died on 27th December, 1979, aged 83 and was buried in Llansardwrnen Churchyard on 31st December. His son, Austin, had pre-deceased him by less than a year.

His writing, shown here, captured the grimness of life for him in the trenches.

Merlin Watts, in his own words

The first section of Merlin's poem in his handwriting is shown illustrated, but a full transcription, as he wrote it, follows:

THIS IS A LITTLE POEM OF 1914-18 WAR

We had to go into the Trenches Ten days & nights without a Break
We was Tired cold and Hungry As we could not get
Our rashens up As the shelling was so bad. Sometimes
It was more than two day before coming up and when
The shelling had dyed a little And when it come we were very
Glad. We had to stand up in trenches there was no place to
Rest But lie up against the back of the Trench and
Hope for the best
When at night we could not have a shit in peace
Them dam mosceatous came bussing around
And sting us about our arse leaving lump so big
As plumbs.
And when the morning came and if it was dry
And light enough to see around all the way down
The line you could see all our comraids with
Their shirts of catching virmin with delight as they
Wanted a bit of peace.
They used to crawl up and down ones Back around ones
Balls and up and down ones Belly enough to drive one
Mad. So we shaved all the hair of our balls for them not
To have anywhere to hid For they might make a raid
And come out and make a raid and strangle poor old Willie
Our feet was tired cold and sore We cannot take our boot
Of We had no place to rest feet for our trench was
Covered with mud and shush and there was no place for one
To rest ones feet and there was nothing we could do.
Autum comes rolling around. With that cold north
Wind and the days are going shorter And the night is
Going longer And that cold North wind will blow
And the nights are dark cold and dreary And some
Times it was snowing and raining and it was
Blowing into our Trench for we had nothing to
Keep it out As it was puting the Trench
Nothing but mud and shush up over our Boots

So we had to stand in that lot our feet was sore
And cold we was standing there like statous
Cold and hungry lyeing against a back of
The Trench proping one and other up sleeping
On ones feet As we could not give our
Livies for a minute or a moment waiting a shell
My drop in our Trenches and Then we
Would be blown to Kingdom Come.

Chapter 4

The War at Sea

LAUGHARNE AND THE WAR AT SEA

When reflecting on the First World War the images and thoughts which are generated usually focus on the Western Front. Well known are the horrors and tragic stories of trench warfare, the enormous loss of life and its impact on communities so, for many, the war is synonymous with Northern France and Belgium. When questioned, other theatres of war may be recalled, e.g. Gallipoli and Palestine. The war at sea is less well known. Most people are aware of the Battle of Jutland, the only significant naval battle of the war, but the role played by both the Royal and Merchant navies throughout the war is little known or appreciated. The Royal Navy kept the German Fleet in port, transported troops, provided hospital ships, supported landings at Gallipoli, prevented essential supplies reaching Germany and escorted convoys of merchant ships bringing essential supplies to Britain and its allies. Such roles were crucial to the survival of the nation and to the successful outcome of the war.

At the outbreak of war Britain had the largest merchant fleet in the world. By the end of the war more than 3,000 British merchant and fishing vessels had been sunk and 15,000 merchant seamen had died. Most received no medals and are not usually commemorated on memorials in communities, although nearly 12,000 names are recorded on the Tower Hill Memorial in London. It commemorates the men of the Merchant Navy and fishing fleets who have no grave but the sea.

From its medieval foundation Laugharne had a port and traded widely. It attracted retired master mariners and it was home to fishermen and sailors. 19th century censuses recorded the widows and wives of sailors. By the outbreak of war the port had declined in significance, but still provided for coastal trade and fishing vessels. The 1911 census still showed people earning a living from the sea and it is not surprising to find that there were Laugharne men who played a role and died in the war at sea.

FIRST CASUALTIES

HMS Hawke.
Courtesy Imperial War Museum.

In October 1914 HMS *Hawke*, a destroyer, was in convoy off the north east coast of Britain. On the morning of the 15th she was hit by a torpedo fired by the German submarine *U-9*. There were nearly 600 men on board and only 70 survived. Amongst those lost were two Laugharne men, Thomas Morgan David and John Arloe Edward Thomas. They were the first sailors from Laugharne to die in the war. Thomas David was born in 1875 and by 1897 he was in the service. He was the son of Thomas and Caroline David of Sand Hills, Laugharne. When he died he had risen to the rank of Engineering Lieutenant Commander. His nephew, Eric Western Wilson, was the only son of Mr JW Western Wilson and Mrs CM Wilson of the Cors. As already seen, sadly, he was the first man from Laugharne to be killed in France on 20th September 1914. John Arloe Edward Thomas, the other fatality, was a leading Carpenter on the *Hawke* and the son of Charles and Martha Thomas of Horsepool Farm.

Captain Price Vaughan Lewes was from Felinfach in Ceredigion. He joined the navy in 1878. He married Anne Josephine Tulloch in 1894. They had a son Martyn Tulloch Vaughan Lewes. The family regularly visited Laugharne and stayed at Hillside with Samitt Willimott and his family. At the outbreak of war Price was on sick leave, though he returned to take command of HMS *Superb*. But he was still unwell and died at Devonport Naval Hospital in November 1914.

Also, in the North Sea a young Laugharne merchant sailor was tasting action for himself when, on 3rd November, his ship, the SS *Eleanor*, which had been carrying supplies to the ill-fated HMS *Hawke* was steaming down the east coast bound for Yarmouth and was attacked by the German fleet. The sailor, Joshua William James Newton, wrote a graphic letter home telling of his experience during the affair, which the *Eleanor* luckily survived. This raid was the first German naval action against the east coast and caused wholesale damage in Yarmouth.

SUBMARINE WARFARE

During the war the submarine became a significant weapon of destruction. In the war German U-Boats sank almost 5,000 ships with a total tonnage of 13 million tons. Initial attacks were in the North Sea, mainly against Royal Navy vessels, HMS *Hawke* being one of the early casualties of this campaign. Merchant vessels were occasionally attacked but not to the extent they were in later years. The British Naval Fleet was considerably larger than the German Fleet and the British Navy was able to blockade German ports preventing resources, including food, getting to the civilian population. In 1915 it was becoming clear that the war would continue for some time. As a result, the German Naval Command, in February 1915, declared the seas around Britain a war zone and would attack all British merchant vessels. Unconditional submarine warfare was launched. This was naval warfare in which submarines sank vessels, such as merchant vessels, without warning, as opposed to attacks per 'Prize rules'. Prize rules had called for submarines to surface and search merchantmen and place crews in a place of safety before sinking their vessel, unless the ship showed 'persistent refusal to stop … or active resistance to visit or search'. The Germans disregarded the law during the First World War following the British introduction of Q-ships with concealed deck guns, so attacks on merchant shipping intensified during 1915.

In a notorious incident the luxury Cunard passenger liner RMS *Lusitania* was torpedoed by German U-boat *U-20* on 7th May, 1915. She was crossing the Atlantic from New York to Liverpool. After a second explosion the ship sank quickly. It went under in 18 minutes, killing 1,200 of almost 2,000 passengers and crew on board. Serving aboard one of the rescue ships, HMS *Juno*, was a young Narberth man, Henry Brynmor John, who would later become a Burgess of Laugharne and Paymaster Lieutenant-Commander with the Royal Navy.

The sinking of RMS *Lusitania* caused international outrage and helped turn public opinion against Germany, particularly in the, then, neutral United States. Of the 1,200 people killed, 128 were American citizens. But the incident did not immediately bring the United States into the war. Instead, the American Government issued a severe protest to Germany. Following immense pressure from the US and recognising the limited effectiveness of the policy, Germany abandoned unrestricted submarine warfare in September 1915.

The sinking of the *Lusitania* became a focus for British and American propaganda and was used to bolster recruitment efforts. However, Germany claimed that the sinking was justified because munitions were being carried on board. In the days prior to the *Lusitania's* final voyage, the German embassy had also published warnings in American newspapers stating the dangers and risks of travelling through the war zone.

The US demanded it stop, and Germany did so. However, Admiral Henning von Holtzendorff, Chief of the Admiralty staff, argued successfully in early 1917 to resume the attacks and thus starve the British. The German high command realized the resumption of unrestricted submarine warfare meant war with the United States but calculated that American mobilization would be too slow to stop a German victory on the Western Front.

ARTHUR WILKINS AND JOHN TUDOR REES GRIFFITH

William Griffith owned the Ship & Castle Inn in King Street and, with his first wife Martha, had five children: four girls and one boy, John Tudor Rees. Martha died in 1897 and two years later William married Elizabeth, the owner of Brown's Hotel on the opposite side of the road. She had a son by her first marriage, Arthur Wilkins, who was the same age as John Tudor Rees.

The two boys grew up together and by 1911 were in a boarding house in Wandsworth where they were both training as telegraph operators. Once trained, John joined the Royal Navy whilst Arthur joined the Merchant Navy.

When war broke out John must have thought he was in the riskier branch, but it turned out that Arthur escaped more action. He had been appointed wireless operator on board the RMS *Lusitania,* and had sailed on her but, luckily, he happened to be home on leave when it set sail from New York in May, 1915. On his next voyage, Arthur's ship was chased by a U-boat across the Atlantic but managed to escape! John on the other hand, seems to have escaped risky action, having become a RNR Warrant Officer, based onshore.

JOHN THOMAS FRANCIS OWEN

John Thomas Francis Owen was born in Clifton Street, Laugharne on 18th May, 1899. He was always known as Francis and was the only son of seven children born to Mary and Thomas Owen, a master mason. In 1903 they moved to live in Victoria Street. Like many other young men in Laugharne he felt the pull of the sea.

Jeff Watt's mother, Hester (Hetty) Watts, was one of Francis Owen's six sisters, and she would tell Jeff about their lives in Laugharne when they were children – before and during the Great War. Hetty told Jeff that from the time Francis was very young he would often say that he wished to join the Royal Navy. In 1912, when he was just 13 years old, Francis told his father that he was going to the RN Recruiting Office in Milford Haven to sign on. He caught the train at St Clears' station, but when he arrived at the Recruiting Office they asked for his birth certificate. He had to return and ask his father to take it to Milford Haven. There the RN's officials told them that Francis was too young to join up, but to apply when he was 15.

So at the age of 15 Francis once again applied to join the Royal Navy and was accepted – just as the Great War began. Hetty said that their mother, Mary, was very worried for him during the war, just like many other parents. In October 1915 Francis was a 'Boy Grade 2' on board the training ship *Impregnable*, a timber ship built in 1860 at Pembroke Dock and immediately made obsolete by newer iron-clad warships. It was based at Devonport, Plymouth. Seven months later he had moved up a grade and in May 1916 transferred to HMS *Princess*. The ship had been a German passenger ship, the *Kronprinzessin Cecilie*, which was captured by the British and converted to an armed merchant cruiser, sailing the coast off East Africa.

In December 1916 Francis became an Ordinary Seaman and in August the following year was transferred to another armed merchant cruiser, HMS *Macedonia,* which gave convoy protection in the South Atlantic seas. Before the end of the war he had been promoted further to Able Seaman. Hetty was under the impression that Francis had been in a fearsome battle. Perhaps there was confusion with HMS *Princess Royal* which did take part in the Battle of Jutland. On convoy duty there was the constant fear of being attacked by U-boats so the ships steered zig-zag courses and remained on high alert throughout the war, which must have been stressful enough.

At times Francis would come home on leave to the great excitement of his family. He would not say a lot to his sisters about his life in the Royal Navy. This was irritating to them. He would however tell his father about his involvement and his life at sea, which must have irritated them even more as their father, Thomas, would not pass the information on! Thomas was a staunch burgess of the Corporation of Laugharne, and extremely keen for his son to become one, too. So in 1920 Thomas arranged for the ceremony to take place over a long weekend's leave at a special court on Saturday, 16th October, 1920.

Francis completed his term of service in the Royal Navy, retiring to join the staff of the Royal Naval College, Dartmouth, where he lived with his wife, Winnie, and three children. But when World War II broke out he re-joined the Royal Navy. He died a year after that war ended, aged only 48, and was cremated at Plymouth on 5th October, 1946. His ashes were returned to Laugharne to join the family grave in St Martin's burial ground.

GALLIPOLI

The German Navy sent their first submarines to the Mediterranean in response to the Anglo-French Dardanelles campaign, after it became obvious that their Austro-Hungarian allies could do little against it with their small submarine force, which nevertheless was successful in defending the Adriatic. The first U-boats sent, *U-21* and the two small coastal boats, *UB-7* and *UB-8*, achieved initial success. *U-21* sank the Royal Navy ships HMS *Triumph* and HMS *Majestic* on 25th and 27th May, respectively, on her way to Constantinople, but ran into severe limitations in the Dardanelles, where swarms of small craft and extensive anti-submarine netting and booms restricted movements.

By the end of June 1915, the Germans had assembled a further three prefabricated submarines at Pola, two of which were to be transferred to the Austrian Navy. They were also assembling three mine-laying submarines, which were ordered converted into transports to carry small quantities of critical supplies to Turkey.

Richard Douglas Stealey was born in 1894 and was a member of the Royal Naval Volunteer Reserve. His father was Captain John Stealey, a retired Master Mariner and his mother was Ada Page Stealey. They lived in Sunny Hill, Holloway Road. Richard was drafted into the Royal Naval Division in September 1914. The Division had been created in August 1914 as there was a shortage of fighting men and not enough ships for Royal Navy sailors. The sailors were formed into eight battalions with naval names. Richard was drafted into the Nelson Battalion. He fought at Gallipoli and on the 3rd May received a head wound. He was evacuated by hospital ship to Alexandria but died of his wounds there on the 7th May. He is buried in Alexandria (Chatby) War Memorial Cemetery.

Another Laugharne sailor killed in the Dardanelles was Thomas Hall Brigstocke. He enlisted in the Royal Navy in 1888. In the 1901 census his mother, Sarah Brigstocke, was living in Gosport Street with her daughter Elizabeth and her granddaughter Mary. Thomas was living in Devonport with his wife, Bessie. He was pensioned off from the Navy in 1910. At the commencement of the war Thomas, as a member of the RNVR, was recalled. He served as Chief Stoker on HMS *Goliath* in the East Indies. In April 1915 she was transferred to the Dardenelles to support the landings. She was attacked on several occasions and was finally sunk by three torpedoes fired by a Turkish torpedo boat. 570 members of her crew including Thomas were lost. He left a widow and eight children and he, sadly, never saw the youngest of them.

THE BATTLE OF JUTLAND

This has been called greatest naval battle the World had ever seen and was also one of the most controversial episodes of the war. Partly because of the rush to cement its position as the most powerful naval force in the world, the Royal Navy had reacted to a naval arms race by Germany in the early years of the twentieth century, as each side battled for supremacy. There was a simmering rivalry between the two navies as to which ruled the waves, the British knowing that they were the greatest naval force, the Germans wishing to be at least their equal.

Apart from some smaller actions at sea during the early stages of the war, no major action had taken place between the British Grand Fleet and the German High Seas Fleet, as both parties were wary of what damage could be caused to them by the other. This situation changed on 31st May, 1916 when the two forces came together in the North Sea off Jutland, with catastrophic results.

There were hundreds of local men serving with the Royal Navy at the time, several of whom served aboard some of the most powerful warships in the world: HMS *Defence*, HMS *Black Prince*, HMS *Indefatigable* and HMS *Invincible*. Confidence ran high throughout both fleets, but at 16.02 hours on 31st May that confidence was shaken among Royal Naval personnel, when the battle-cruiser *Indefatigable* blew to smithereens after suffering direct hits in her magazines, taking 1,010 men to the bottom in minutes. Soon afterwards the *Defence* blew up, and the loss the *Invincible* followed with all but six of her crew. 15 Carmarthenshire men were lost aboard these ships; seven aboard the *Indefatigable*, five on the *Defence*, two aboard the *Invincible* and one on the *Black Prince*. Among the dead was Stuart Bladen Nelson Bolton, of Elm House, King Street, Laugharne. At least three other men from Laugharne are known to have fought at Jutland and survived: Arthur James Evans, of Halfpenny Furze, who was aboard HMS *Marlborough*; and Bridgman Rochfort Mordaunt-Smith, of Milton Bank, who was aboard HMS *Colossus*, were two of them.

David John had been born in Hugdon cottage, the Lacques. He was one of at least seven, possibly up to 10 children, born to John and Esther Lewis (nee Roblin). David had been in the Navy since 1902, and by the outbreak of war, was a gunner on the dreadnought, HMS *St Vincent*. During the battle of Jutland, shells fired from the *St Vincent* hit the light cruiser SMS *Wiesbaden*, and later twice made direct hits on the battlecruiser SMS *Moltke* before it disappeared into the mist. David was the third Laugharne survivor.

Whilst Jutland could be described as a draw, in fact the British aim was achieved, as the German High Seas Fleet never went to sea again during the war.

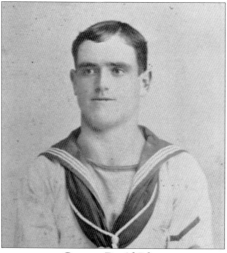

Gunner David John.

*HMS Indefatigable sinking after being hit by two shells
which caused a further devastating explosion.*
Courtesy Imperial War Museum.

UNRESTRICTED SUBMARINE WARFARE

In December 1916, Admiral von Holtzendorff composed a memorandum supporting Germany's resumption, in 1917, of unrestricted U-boat warfare. Holtzendorff proposed breaking Britain's resistance by sinking 600,000 tons of shipping per month. This was based on a study that stated that if merchant shipping was sunk at such a rate, Britain would run out of shipping and be forced to sue for peace within six months, well before the Americans could act. Holtzendorff assured the Kaiser

> I give your Majesty my word as an officer, that not one American will land on the Continent.

In January 1917, the Kaiser met with key staff to discuss measures to resolve Germany's increasingly grim war situation. Its military campaign in France had stalled and with Allied divisions outnumbering Germany's by 190 to 150, a successful Allied offensive was a possibility. The German Navy was bottled up in its home port and the British blockade had caused a food scarcity that was causing civilian deaths due to malnutrition. The military staff urged the Kaiser to unleash the submarine fleet. On 31st January, the Kaiser signed the order for unrestricted submarine warfare to resume.

Britain's Admiral Beatty commented that:

> The real crux lies in whether we blockade the enemy to his knees, or whether he does the same to us.

Germany had 105 submarines ready for action and new construction ensured that, despite losses, at least 120 submarines would be available for the rest of 1917. The campaign was initially a great success, nearly 500,000 tons of shipping being sunk in both February and March, and 860,000 tons in April. Britain had only six weeks' supplies of wheat remaining. In May losses exceeded 600,000 tons, and in June 700,000.

On 3rd February, in response to the new submarine campaign, President Wilson severed all diplomatic relations with Germany, and the US Congress declared war on 6th April, 1917.

LEVI REES DAVIES

Levi was born in 1891 at Rogers Well, Llansadwrnen. In 1911 he was recorded as an iron founder and joined the Navy during the war. As there were more men than ships needing them, he was seconded to the Merchant Navy as an engineer.

Levi Rees Davies and his wife Sarah Jane Evans.
Courtesy R G Davies.

His older sister, Penelope, was born in 1887. She became a nurse in Swansea General and Eye Hospital, St Helen's Road – one of 22 caring for 126 patients. During the war she nursed in Mesopotamia. Penny eventually married a Canadian doctor, George Shanks, and went to live in Vancouver.

Levi eventually became a Chief Engineer. On 17th February, 1917 his ship 'Iolo' (3,840 tons) was sunk off the south of Ireland, 40 miles southwest of Fastnet. She had been sailing from Cardiff to La Spezia in Italy with coal. There were two casualties and the Master, Chief Engineer and two gunners were taken prisoner by the U-60 under Commander Karlgeorg Schuster. Levi and the rest of the crew landed safely in Ireland. He was awarded the Mercantile Marine War Medal and ribbon and the British War Medal. He survived the war and retired from the sea 1939, he then farmed Mapsland Farm, Laugharne, until his death in 1946.

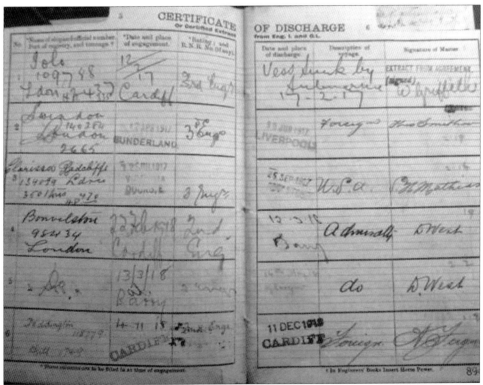

Levi Davies' discharge papers. The first entry on the page is for the SS Iolo. Note the reason for discharge!

Alfred John, a brother of David John who was at Jutland, was also already serving – in the Royal Marines Light Infantry. Affy, as he was known, served aboard HMS *Idaho* which was the official name given to the Auxiliary Patrol Base at Milford Haven. It took its name from a requisitioned steam yacht – 43 tons (gross) built in 1910. She was taken over by the Navy on 12th April, 1915 and fitted with a heavy machine gun for use as a patrol vessel against submarines.

Alfred "Affy" John.

Sidney Allen was born in Begelly, Pembrokeshire and joined his father and brothers as a collier when he left school at the age of 14. In his late teens he met Evelyn James, daughter of John and Esther James, who lived in Laugharne, and they were married on 16th September, 1916 at St Martin's church, and afterwards lived at Broadway Lodge.

Sid joined the Royal Navy at Devonport on 10th May, 1918. Soon after he left to serve with the Navy, his wife found that she was expecting their second child. Florence, was born in January 1919, and was two months old by the time Sid came home to Broadway.

Sid served in HMS *Vivid II*, which was the shore training base at Devonport, until September 1918, completing training as a Stoker 2nd class. A stoker's job was physically hard, continually shovelling coal into the boiler to power the ship and especially when full steam ahead was required. It was also dusty and hot. Stokers often wore hessian masks to prevent their face from being burnt by the intense heat. This kind of physical labour was something Sid would have been used to in his former work as a miner.

From September to December 1918 he, too, served on HMS *Idaho* now based at Killiney in Ireland during this period. The *Idaho* would have been used mainly in anti-submarine patrols and to escort merchant shipping. During his time aboard, *Idaho* sailed as far south as Gibraltar and San Sebastian in Spain and Sid sent postcards home to his wife and eldest daughter, Eileen, who had been born in August 1917.

From January 1919 until his demobilisation in March, he served on HMS *Satellite*, a steam corvette of 1,420 tons built in 1881 and used as a base ship, located on the Tyne. His conduct throughout his service is recorded as very good. He was awarded the 1914-1918 Victory and War Medal.

When Sid came home from the Navy he returned to working in the mines, at the Ocean colliery, Nantymoel in the Ogmore Valley, only coming home every couple of months. In December 1921 a third child was born to Sid and Evelyn, a boy, named Roy.

When the Second World War began, Sid joined up once again, this time in the Army. He served in the 17th battalion of the Welch Regiment from December 1939 until August 1941 when he was invalided out. He did not serve overseas but remained in Wales. He was awarded the 1939-45 War Medal.

Afterwards he found employment at the newly established MOD Proof and Experimental Establishment at Pendine, until his retirement in 1962. Sid continued living in Broadway Lodge until his death on 19th May, 1978, in Glangwili Hospital. He was cremated at Parcgwyn and his ashes placed in the family grave at Llansadurnen churchyard.

Sidney Allen.

While submarines waited for potential targets off the south coast of Ireland they brought the war experience into the Irish Sea and up the Bristol Channel. Part of this submarine warfare occurred just off the Welsh coast. Ships entering and leaving ports all around the Welsh coast, and others destined for Liverpool and Manchester, were attacked. There were some 170 losses of early aircraft and shipping around the Welsh coast comprising some large merchant ships and naval vessels, passenger vessels, as well as smaller fishing vessels and coastal traders. Many of the smaller harbours of the Welsh coast and their communities have links to a 'lost ship' and a lost sailor from the war.

Walking around many churchyards in coastal areas of Wales, it is quite likely that you will come across the grave of a sailor who had been found washed ashore locally and buried in a 'Sailor's Plot', either under a named headstone, or marked simply as an 'Unknown Sailor'.

Some cemeteries contain the familiar white Portland headstone marking the grave of sailors who were casualties of war and these were erected by the Commonwealth War Graves Commission (CWGC) to mark the last resting place of the poor sailor buried beneath.

St Martin's Churchyard in Laugharne contains a small plot which contains the graves of several sailors whose bodies had been recovered from Laugharne Sands over the years.

On 8th February, 1918, a local man and coastguard, Frank Brown, walking at the Ginst Point spotted a small lifeboat which had run ashore. He was shocked to discover the bullet riddled body of a sailor lying in the bottom, and he called the local Policeman, PC Hoare. An inquest into the death of the man was held by the County Coroner, Mr Thomas Walters, who found that the man had died as a result of a gunshot wound to the head. Among the papers in the man's pockets was an Alien's Registration Card, which had been stamped several times by the Carmarthenshire Constabulary and this enabled the body to be identified as that of a Venezuelan sailor, Domingo Mobile.

Domingo served with the Mercantile Marine aboard the London registered steamship, S.S. *Sofie*, which had been built in 1907. On 1st February, 1918 she was en-route from Jersey to Cardiff in ballast when she was attacked in the Bristol Channel by the German submarine *U-101*. She was hit by gunfire from the surfaced U-Boat and went down with the loss of eight lives: Hubert Francis Burdett (Master), aged 22, of Frampton-on-Severn; C. Amesti (Fireman), aged 46, of Bilbao; John Bernard Harrington (Mate), aged 27, of Barry; William George Lippiatt (First Engineer), aged 56, of Bristol; Devanez Martinez (Second

The lifeboat that Domingo was found in was kept and is shown in this photograph moored to the left of the Lena at Laugharne. It was broken up in the 1950s.
Courtesy of D. Brown.

Engineer), aged 30, of Newport; Peter Soper (Fireman), aged 35, of Venzuala; Ormond Stevens (Able Seaman), aged 33, of Guernsey; and Domingo Mobile.

Domingo was 39 years old when he was killed and he was buried in St Martin's Churchyard, Laugharne on 13th February, 1918. Details regarding his burial were not passed on to the authorities, so after the war his body was assumed to have been lost at sea and his name was included on the Tower Hill Memorial, in London.

However, local war historian, Steve John, discovered that Domingo's burial had been recorded in the burial register at St Martin's Church. This prompted him to carry out some more research in order to gather evidence to present to the Commonwealth War Graves Commission (CWGC), in order to gain Domingo a proper headstone. This evidence was presented to them and they quickly accepted it, altering his details in their online Book of Remembrance.

On Thursday the 4th May, 2017, the CWGC erected a 'Special Memorial' headstone in the Churchyard to commemorate Domingo. So after almost a hundred years of lying in an unmarked grave, Domingo Mobile now has a CWGC headstone to mark his last resting place!

The lifeboat was re-named the Domingo and for many years it was used in Laugharne. It appears in photographs and postcards of the old port of Laugharne and the estuary of the Corran.

While there is no way to know for certain, other bodies washed ashore at Laugharne were probably those of other incidents of unrestricted submarine warfare.

The Carmarthen Journal of 17th August 1917 reported:

> The body of an unknown person...in such an advanced state of decom-position as to be beyond recognition, was found on Tuesday morning on Laugharne Sands by Sergeant Wilfred Morgan, ASC. He informed PC Warmington and they both conveyed the body to a shed at Great Hill farm...An open verdict was returned.

Another body of a sailor was washed up at Laugharne and caused something of an embarrassment to the County Council, which was reported in *The Carmarthen Journal* of 9th November, 1917:

> It is much to be regretted that whilst sailors are losing their lives daily to keep us supplied with food that local authorities should quarrel over a bill of £4 for burying the body of an "unknown man" washed up at Laugharne. Unfortunately, the bodies of unknown men are washed up on every coast of Britain just now.

The Registrar had ordered the burial in St Martin's churchyard of this uniden-tified sailor whose body had been recovered from Laugharne Sands the previous week, but the County Council initially refused to pay for the cost of the burial, until being embarrassed to do so by newspaper reports such as this.

The bodies of these known and unknown sailors washed ashore at Laugharne brought the reality and proximity of the war to local communities. The trenches of the Western Front were hundreds of miles away – the war at sea was happening on the doorstep. Laugharne was no exception and all around the Welsh coast bodies and debris from the casualties of warfare at sea were being washed ashore. While far fewer men from Laugharne were killed at sea than in other theatres of war, sacrifices were made. Food and other resources got through to the civilian population, but thousands of Royal and Merchant Navy sailors died to ensure that this happened.

Chapter 5

Belgian Refugees in Laugharne

'IT WAS THE LARGEST INFLUX OF REFUGEES IN BRITISH HISTORY
BUT IT'S A STORY THAT IS ALMOST TOTALLY IGNORED'
(TONY KUSHNER, PROFESSOR OF MODERN HISTORY
AT THE UNIVERSITY OF SOUTHAMPTON.)

When Germany invaded neutral Belgium on 4th August, 1914, and Britain declared war on Germany stories about atrocities by the German troops on Belgian citizens quickly spread there and many fled their homes. Eventually about 1.5 million people sought refuge abroad. Initially more than a million went to the Netherlands, about 325,000 refugees went to France, most of whom stayed there throughout the war, and roughly a quarter of a million Belgians crossed the Channel to Britain.

Belgian refugees began to arrive in Britain at the end of August 1914 and the numbers increased throughout the year. By the middle of 1915 there were well over 250,000 refugees nationally including 40,000 wounded soldiers. Initial shelter was found in places like Alexandra Palace and Earls Court in London but this was only temporary.

Appeals were made in newspapers and in letters to chairmen of county councils, urban district councils and mayors and, in response, 2,500 local voluntary committees were formed offering relief and accommodation. People even offered rooms in their own homes. Churches also helped.

The refugees, 'plucky little Belgians', were initially greeted with open arms and the Government used their plight to encourage anti-German sentiment and public support for the war but, as time went on, some friction did arise. The different habits and customs of the Belgians caused many arguments. The women did not wear hats in public and alcohol consumption happened out in the open. However, that was nothing compared to the 'barbaric' habit of eating horse meat. This met with a wall of disapproval from the British. In addition, the presence of able-bodied men caused resentment until the munitions crisis of 1916 when several thousand refugees were employed in the new factories, some of which were Belgian owned and managed.

In Wales, there were over 4,500 refugees hosted all over the country; more than 1,000 in Pembrokeshire, about 250 in Carmarthenshire and around 1,500 in Glamorgan. Many of those in Pembrokeshire arrived by fishing boat at Milford Haven, having escaped via Ostend. In all, 26 boats, two of which carried the staff and pupils of the Belgian Royal IBIS School, brought the refugees. Some stayed for the duration of the war where they were first received, some moved to other parts of Britain to work, some went to Holland or France, and some returned to Belgium.

When the war ended in November 1918, most refugees returned to Belgium, although not immediately. The organised return lasted well into 1919, with skilled workers returning first. They returned to a country where the infrastructure was destroyed and where unemployment was high.

Some 5,000 Belgians chose to remain in Britain, having married British people or made a new life here. For example, in Laugharne are the descendants of Florimond Rasson and Charles and Bertha Deschoolmeester, who originally came from Ostend. But, other than some memorial tablets, wooden carvings such as those at Llanfihangel y Creuddyn Church and Llanwenog School's war memorial, and the Anglo Belgian War Memorial in London, there is little to show that Britain played host to such a significant number of refugees during World War One.

Details of the refugees who came to Laugharne are sketchy. We know that there were two families: Florent Vandervoort, his wife and children, Edmond and Louisa; M. and Madame Demoulin, their daughter in law, and small grandson, René; plus two single women: Mlles Goormans and Couynans, who may have been relatives of Madame Demoulin. They were later joined by a male relative, Anthony Couynans. Nearby St Clears hosted one family and Pendine also hosted 'a few'.

PREPARATIONS FOR ARRIVAL

Preparations for the hosting of refugees in Laugharne began in November 1914 after the national appeal. The Portreeve, W.E. Edwards, called a public meeting the purpose of which was 'to receive reports of the collectors of funds and furniture.' Collectors raised £6. 11s. ½d in the first week and promises of furniture 'ranging from whole suites to individual cooking utensils' were ample. By the end of November, a Belgian Refugees Committee had been formed with the Portreeve appointed Chairman, Samuel David as Secretary and Mrs Peel, Fernhill, as Treasurer.

Richard Pearce, New Shop, wrote to *The Welshman* offering two houses rent-free for a year; one on the Grist with eight rooms and another with two rooms. In addition, B.R. Thomas and Henry Raymond offered houses, the former in Duncan Street. After heated discussions, it was finally agreed that the Committee would pay an allowance of 12s. 6d to each married couple and 2s. 6d for each child. At a meeting at the end of November a decision to apply for two families of five was made. However, a letter from headquarters reported that:

> ...no refugees were in need of accommodation at present, but large numbers were expected from Holland soon.

ARRIVAL AT LAUGHARNE

On each of two occasions in early December preparations were made to receive two families but neither arrived. However, on 12th December news was received in Laugharne that eight people were due to arrive at St Clears station. It was reported that:

> Large numbers of people assembled at various points in town to welcome them...but no refugees appeared.

The Grist, Laugharne.

Eventually they arrived by motor from Carmarthen at 11pm. and were received at Mr Pearce's house on the Grist. The two families, Demoulin and Vanderwoort, had been neighbours at Berchem, a suburb of Antwerp and had escaped the city together.

FLEEING ANTWERP

The experiences of these two families would have been very similar to that of Jacques De Hont, a Belgian refugee living at Bridgend, whose detailed account of the fall of Antwerp on October 9th, 1914 was printed in *The Glamorgan Gazette* on October 30th, 1914.

> Antwerp, or a great part of it is in ruins....Bombs fell on all parts of the city, and shells overhead were screaming as they tore their way through the air....Houses were struck until nothing remained but bare walls ....Flames sprang up to the sky from those houses where shells had fallen.
>
> Near my house I found my brother and wife had already left, with thousands of others, who were making their way to the Dutch frontier. We left our home and almost immediately after we saw it fall in a heap of ruins as a shell struck it. Immediately after another hit the hospital....
>
> Antwerp was in flames....Crowds of people were to be seen rushing along the street carrying the possessions they had managed to secure wrapped up in sheets and slung over their shoulders.
>
> Little children clung to their mothers' skirts crying and screaming ....old men and old women, feeble and infirm, were trying to keep up with the others, but hundreds had to fall behind. Most of them were making for the Dutch frontier.
>
> ....On the way we passed thousands of others. Some had no hats, many of the women were carrying their boots....all were trying to comfort the others.

Initially the Demoulin family were housed on the Grist and the Vandervoorts in the Duncan Street property.

In a letter to Mr David, Monsieur Vandervoort described his family's arrival in Laugharne:

138

Belgian refugees fleeing Antwerp.

I cannot help referring back to our arrival ten months ago, 12th December 1914. Like shipwrecked people, long tossed by the storm, we wandered as chance chased from our home by the detested invader, not knowing whither fate would lead us when our good star led us to Laugharne. In spite of the late hour and even of the weather, you did not hesitate an instant to sacrifice a portion of the night in order to receive your refugees, to strengthen them with kind words inspired by warm and cordial sympathy. We at once felt that we had arrived at a good harbour and that we had come to the end of our trials and sorrows...

(Florent Vandervoort: November 1915, *Carmarthen Journal, Laugharne News*).

The newcomers were 'hospitably entertained during the festive season' with several locals providing gifts, coal, potatoes and vegetables and, at the New Year's Eve Ball, hosted by Mrs Peel, Fern Hill, M. Florent Vanderwoort thanked Laugharne people for the kindness that they had received so far.

Samuel Thomas with Madame Demoulin, her daughter in law and grandson,
René and one other outside the Grist House.

René (possibly at Pendine).

On the 12th February, *The Welshman* reported that:

> There are now 12 refugees in Laugharne; the husband and daughter of Madame Demoulin and two other relatives.

It was also reported that many were 'rapidly acquiring our language'. The Committee were now responsible for payments of £2 15s weekly with promised subscriptions reported to be 'satisfactory'.

Nestor Demoulin, an 'automobile driver' in the Belgian Army, visited his family frequently. In March 1915, Mr Tyler, the Headteacher of Laugharne School, noted in the school log book that:

> The children were very privileged to see this afternoon German helmets, caps, great coats, cartridges and portions of shells which had been brought here by a Belgian soldier whose wife is a local refugee.

In addition his father made some 'interesting articles' from cartridges and other articles brought by his son from the Flanders battlefields. Nestor was also able to give local people a vivid description of his experiences, including a 'hair's breadth escape'.

Edmond and Louisa Vanderwoort at Letchworth,
December 1916.

Nestor Demoulin.

The Kryn & Lahy metalworks at Letchworth.

On 25th May 1915, *The Welshman* reported that:

> In future families should be paid a weekly sum for their maintenance and that the committee make no payment outside that amount. It was agreed that each family should receive 26s weekly and in the case of the individual lady 10 shillings weekly.

At the same time permission was given for Monsieur Demoulin to look for work.

Refugees who were fit for work were encouraged and supported to do so. One of the single young women worked locally and in May 1915, Anthony

Couynans started work as an electrical engineer at Briton Ferry Steelworks, a business owned by Mr Eccles of Broadway Mansion. Shortly afterwards Monsieur Demoulin found employment with Henry Raymond of Honeycorse at a wage of £1 a week.

In October 1915 the Vandervoort family moved to Letchworth where Florent was employed at a large Belgian-owned munitions factory. They were awarded £25 by the Laugharne Committee 'towards the expenses of furnishing a house'.

The Laugharne correspondent of *The Welshman* reported that the children had 'made numerous friends' at the local school which they attended and that 'their fellow pupils much regretted their removal'.

Ladies and Gentlemen,

In the name of my husband, my children and myself, I thank you once more with all my heart for the kindness that you have done for us. Your generosity in helping us to make comfortable the new home which we are about to establish at Letchworth is the crowning point of all the benefits that you have done for us. We will never forget it and hope if the circumstances do not permit us to come and bid you goodbye before returning definitely to our Belgian home, will be to receive you with all welcome at our home and of proving to you to the utmost of our power that we shall regard you throughout our life with deepest gratitude. Thus it will not be, ladies and gentlemen, goodbye but "Au Revoir" until better times.

M Vandervoort.

At around the same time Mlle Couynans was given £15 by the Committee 'as a dowry' as she was leaving Laugharne to get married. Similarly, in November, Mlle Goormans went to Holland to be married.

Her future husband was a Belgian soldier, who has found employment as a clerk in an office.
(*Carmarthen Journal* Oct 29th, 1915)

With these departures, the only Belgians remaining in Laugharne were the family Demoulin at a time when subscriptions were declining. It was reported that monthly collections now amounted to about half the original sum.

That leaves us with only one Belgian family to help to support, so the call on the purses of the subscribers in future will not be so heavy.

Total collections to December 1915 were reported to be £224. 4s 8½d with a current balance of £19 10s 3d. Unfortunately, Monsieur Demoulin had needed to give up work as his wife was seriously ill.

DEATH OF MADAME DEMOULIN

In Laugharne Churchyard, near to the main entrance of the church, there is a distinctive grave; a simple wooden cross with the words:

> Leonie Sohy Demoulin
> A Notre mere
> Regrettée

The day following her death, the Refugee Committee held a special meeting at which it was agreed that all expenses should be paid for by the Committee. However, it soon transpired that Dr V.Ll. Jones of St Clears, who had treated Madame Demoulin throughout her illness, had given his services free so there were only funeral expenses to pay. These were later stated to be £11 9s 8½d.

The funeral took place at St Martin's Church on Thursday, 20th January, 1916 and was conducted in French according to the rites of the Roman Catholic Church by Father Xavier, a Belgian priest staying at Milford Haven. *The Welshman* reported that 'the funeral was very largely attended' with the chief mourners being her husband, her son, Madame De Gorman and Madame Black. At the graveside Father Xavier addressed the crowd in English and French. He thanked the people present for 'their sympathy and charity towards our poor Belgian people' and prayed that Madame Demoulin would 'receive the reward of those who fulfil their duties faithfully'.

Monsieur Demoulin left Laugharne soon after the funeral, whether to return to Belgium we do not know, but he was awarded £5 in travel expenses by the Committee. At the beginning of February, Mrs Brayshay, of the Glen, received a letter in which he expressed his deep gratitude for the benefits received by him and his family and stating that he 'would never forget the kindness shown by the people of Laugharne'. Now there were only four refugees left; Madame Demoulin the younger, her son René and two single women. They were moved from the house on the Grist to Platform Cottage, Clifton Street, with the rent paid by Mrs Peel, of Fernhill.

*This is the grave, with its original cross, of Madame Leonie Demoulin
who died of heart failure aged 58 at Grist House,
on January 17th 1916, after 'a long illness'.*

Mrs Peel.

Platform House with Platform Cottage alongside.

L to R: Madam Demoulin (daughter in law), Ada Thomas, Margaret Griffith,
Mrs Thomas & Samuel Thomas. Front: René Demoulin, Dora Thomas.

Nestor Demoulin 1914/15.

GROWING TENSIONS

As the effects of the war on the community became greater and people had to endure more hardships, some locals began to resent the money spent on their Belgian guests. There was news of deaths and injuries at the front and, at home, Laugharne folks were raising money for the Red Cross, organising Christmas boxes for 'their boys', working hard to produce more food locally, collecting eggs for the war effort and beginning to feel the effects of butter shortages. In addition, many local women were now doing jobs previously done by men.

In September 1916, it was questioned whether an allowance should be paid to the two refugees (unnamed) while they were away on holiday. There was also 'general discontent' about the weekly allowance paid to 'the single able-bodied woman who ought, it is thought, be earning her own living'. The main argument for this was that many of the subscribers had their own daughters who'd had to go into domestic service. By the following March, 1917, it was reported in *The Welshman* that the single lady had taken a paid domestic post with a Belgian family at Carmarthen.

Christmas 1917 brought further resentment. At the beginning of January a special meeting of the Refugee Committee was called to discuss a request that a Belgian family living at Pendine be moved to Laugharne. Miss Cunningham reported that they had been 'quite destitute' on Christmas Day, news which surprised many people, and it soon transpired that they had not been destitute at all; quite the opposite as the husband was in regular employment and the son was in receipt of six shillings a week. In addition, the local Committee provided a reasonable amount of weekly groceries, free coal and a house rent-free. The incident caused bad feeling between various parties in Laugharne and Pendine, the upshot being that the family were moved to Laugharne to 'be maintained by Mr Eccles' (of Broadway).

On February 2nd, 1917, *The Welshman* printed a notice on their correspondence page:

> We thank "Laugharnite" for his letter during the Laugharne Refugee outrage but as we are of the opinion that if it is published it may lead to more friction and aggravate matters we must respectfully refrain from printing it.
> Ed *"Welshman"*

By the middle of March 1917, Madame Demoulin, the younger, and her son were the only Belgians dependent on the Committee and it was decided that an allowance of 17s 6d per week, rent free, was generous as she 'has a husband who is able to visit them from Belgium'.

DAILY LIFE AND REPATRIATION

We know little about the lives of this young woman and her son over the next two years. Did René start in Laugharne School? Did his mother take part in social activities or contribute to the war effort? We may never know. However, we do know that she and her family remained forever grateful to the people of Laugharne, and maybe to Miss Cunningham and Samuel Thomas in particular because she kept in touch with both at least until the next invasion of Belgium, in 1940.

The young Madame Demoulin and René finally left Laugharne on March 17th, 1919, probably with the Carmarthen Belgians who had been living at Rhydygors. It was reported that they boarded a large charabanc in Carmarthen at 4.30am for Swansea, where they joined other refugees en route for Tilbury Docks, sailing for Antwerp on the *'Guilford Castle'*. At Carmarthen there had been a farewell ceremony with the planting of a horn beech tree by the oldest Belgian refugee as a thank you to the people of Carmarthen. The report in *The Welshman* was positive and informative. However the Laugharne News section that same week simply reported that:

> The last of the Belgian refugees domiciled at Laugharne left early this week.

Just over two years later, in September 1921, Samuel Thomas and the Portreeve of Laugharne, William Clarke Griffith, visited Belgium, perhaps at the invitation of the Demoulin and Vandervoort families. Again, the newspaper report was frustratingly brief:

> The retiring Portreeve of Laugharne, William Clarke Griffith, has just returned from a tour of France and Belgium.
> (*The Welshman*, October 7th, 1921)

However, thanks to Rosemary Rees's family photographs we know that they met with Madame Demoulin and viewed the devastation in Belgium.

Samuel Thomas, René Demoulin, William Clarke Griffith, Belgium.
September 1921.

Ruins of the Flour Mill at Dixmude/Diksmuide, Belgium.
September 1921.

THE DESCHOOLMEESTERS: THE FAMILY WHO STAYED

Bertha and Charles (Carlo) Deschoolmeester fled from Ostend in Belgium with their five children as the Germans advanced in August 1914. They crossed the channel in one of Charles' father's trawlers, arriving at Folkestone on 28th September. To ensure that they did not get lost, the children were linked to their parents by strings which were tied around their wrists. First, the family were sent to the Alexandra Palace Reception Centre in North London and from there to Llanegwad near Nantgaredig. It is thought that they may have asked to go to South Wales because Bertha's brother, Leon, was one of the Ostend trawler men who had recently been evacuated with his family to Milford Haven.

The Deschoolmeesters finally arrived at Llanegwad on November 3rd, 1914 where a house had been prepared for them by the local Belgian Refugee Committee.

> All along the route from the station the men, women and children showed their welcome by waving hands and the display of the Belgian flag and Union Jack.
> *Carmarthen Journal* November 20th, 1914

It was reported that the Belgian family were living in a five-roomed house, Llwyn y Bryn, which was owned by Mrs Bath, Alltyferin, the Quaker wife of a prominent Swansea industrialist. The house had been furnished by donations from local people.

Soon after that the following notice was placed in *La Belgique*, a newspaper for Belgians living in Britain:

> Fam Schoolmeester se trouve a Llanegwad, Nantgaredig, Carmarthen.
> (*The Schoolmeester family can be found at Nantgaredig, Carmarthen.*)

We can only surmise as to the relief Bertha and Charles must have felt on being settled because the birth of their sixth child was imminent; on 8th December 1914, Egwad, was born, his name a tribute to the people who welcomed the family into their community.

On 17th January, 1916, there was a concert in aid of the Belgian refugees at Alltyferin, Llanegwad at which:

> a striking feature was the rendering of the Belgian National Anthem by Mr De Schoolmeester.
> (*Cothi Bridge News, Carmarthen Journal*)

As with many other Belgian people, Charles was employed during the war. A news article in *The Carmarthen Journal*, 4th August, 1916, names him as a mechanic at The Central Garage, Nott Square, Carmarthen. In May 1918, they moved to Maesycoed, Abergwili when Charles was earning £3 5s a week as a mechanic. In December he was warned by the school attendance officer that he had to send his children to school regularly. In her defence, Bertha had stated that she could not afford to clothe all seven children and Charles said that his wages were due to increase to £4 shortly so he could ensure that his children attended regularly in future. (*Carmarthen Journal*, December 6th, 1918).

Sometime later Charles worked at the St Clears Milk Factory as an electrical engineer and in May 1920 the family moved to St Clears, firstly living at Reigate House, Station Road and later next door at Oaklands, which they bought for £350.

For whatever reason, Charles and Bertha did not return to Belgium when the Great War ended, choosing instead to live and raise their family in St Clears, perhaps because Belgium had been totally devastated and unemployment was high. Altogether they had eleven children: Leone, Pierre, Carlo (Charles), Yvonne, Marie, Robert (Bob) (all Belgian born), Egwad, Irene, Etienne, Jack (Jacques) and Bernadette.

The Family outside Reigate House, Station Rd, St Clears 1922.
Bertha and Charles with Yvonne, Irene, Marie, Pierre,
Leone, Robert (Bob), Egwad, Charles (Carlo).

The Family at Charles' funeral in December 1953.
L to R: Bernadette, Yvonne, Robert, Egwad, Bertha, Jacques, Marie,
Charles, Pierre, Etienne, Leone. (Irene was away)

Bertha was a staunch Catholic and regularly attended St Mary's Catholic Church in Carmarthen. She was also a skilful needlewoman and often made things to sell for church funds. Charles continued to work at the Milk Factory until his retirement. He died in 1952 and Bertha in 1976. They are buried in Carmarthen Cemetery.

Leone, the eldest son, worked at Lowndes Garages in Carmarthen until he was 70. Unlike his Belgian born brothers, he was exempt from serving in World War II because he was a mechanic. Leone was granted British citizenship in 1947. He did return to Ostend where he was born for a visit with his own family and was able to find the house where the family had lived years before. Leone lived most of his life in Carmarthen and St Clears and is buried with his wife Olwen in Llanfihangel Abercywyn Churchyard.

Etienne settled at Cross Inn, Laugharne. He worked as an electrician at the Proof and Experimental Establishment (PEE), Pendine for many years and some of his descendants still live locally.

FLORIMOND RASSON AND SARAH EDMUNDS: A BELGIAN-WELSH WEDDING

Florimond and Sarah with their son, Ronald.
(photo: James Beynon)

On 7th July, 1917, Sarah Edmunds, a member of a well-known Laugharne family, married Florimond Rasson at Carmarthen Registry Office. It was reported that the couple were given a 'rousing reception at Laugharne on their return, the streets being gaily decorated with flags etc.'

Florimond was born on a farm at Wodecque, Belgium in 1889 and had served in the Belgian Infantry but he was wounded at the front line and, like 40,000 other Belgian soldiers, sent to this country for treatment. He met Sarah whilst he was at Pendine recuperating and she was working at Honeycorse Farm. Although he was not a refugee, he developed a strong friendship with Miss Cunningham of the Refugee Committee and Henry Raymond, Honeycorse, who employed him at his quarry. After the war he returned briefly to Belgium to obtain his military discharge and to facilitate his British naturalisation but, otherwise, he lived in Victoria Street, Laugharne with Sarah and their four children for the rest of his life. He died in 1946 and his daughter in 2018, aged 99. His grandson still lives in Laugharne.

Chapter 6

Caring for the Wounded

THE STORY OF LAUGHARNE'S NURSES

Long before the first shots were fired by British troops in the Great War, the Government had made plans, in the event of a future war abroad, for wounded soldiers to be treated in hospitals back in Britain. As part of this plan, across England and Wales Voluntary Aid Detachments (known as VADs) were formed on 16th August, 1909. Organised by the British Red Cross and the Order of St John, their role was to assist the Government in wartime by helping the territorial medical service. VADs were eventually formed in every county. Voluntary membership grew quickly with the outbreak of war and a Joint Committee was formed on 24th August, 1914, between the Red Cross and St John's, in order to work together, raising funds and sharing resources.

The Red Cross had searched for suitable properties for use as hospitals and convalescent homes prior to the Declaration of War, so as soon as wounded men began to arrive, these hospitals were made ready with equipment and staff in place. They were known as 'auxiliary hospitals', which came under the umbrella of a central military hospital. In Wales the main military hospital was located in Cardiff. There were over 3,000 auxiliary hospitals in the UK.

Wounded soldiers were initially treated at dressing stations close to the front line, then taken to casualty clearing stations further behind the front line, and from there transported to 'base hospitals', or 'stationary hospitals', well behind the front lines, near to railway stations and ports, ready to take men back to 'blighty', to a military or specialist hospital, or an auxiliary hospital, depending on their medical needs. In Carmarthenshire there were four auxiliary hospitals: two in Llandovery, one in Llanelli and one in Carmarthen. These auxiliary hospitals had a Commandant in overall charge, and a Matron who directed the nursing staff and members of the VAD. The soldiers treated at these hospitals were not those with the most serious injuries, but were quite often recovering from bullet and shrapnel wounds or suffering various illnesses, and in need of convalescence. Many preferred the auxiliary hospitals to the military hospital because they were not as strict and the surroundings were generally more pleasant, many being in country houses with large gardens. However, the solders still remained under military control and would be returned to their unit once fit.

Just 10 days after war began *The Carmarthen Journal* reported that the Carmarthenshire Branch of the British Red Cross Society was making extensive preparations throughout the county to cope with all possible contingencies. The Governors of the Carmarthen Infirmary had decided to equip 12 beds at the infirmary, and more if necessary, for war wounded. These men would be regarded as patients of the Infirmary and nursed by Infirmary staff. In addition the Infirmary would allow up to four trained nurses to volunteer their services to the Red Cross to work as nurses outside the Infirmary. It was also agreed that the Infirmary could be used as a depot for the Red Cross to receive medical, surgical and other supplies for distribution and that the board-room of the Infirmary could be used for meetings of the Red Cross. On 6th November it was reported that the military authorities had ordered the auxiliary Red Cross Hospital at 1, Penlan Road in Carmarthen (located in the "new" building of the workhouse), to be opened in readiness to receive sick and wounded soldiers at any time. On 20th November the first group of 44 wounded soldiers arrived in Carmarthen, eight were placed in the Infirmary and 36 in the Red Cross Hospital. As the war continued and the casualties mounted, so the demand for beds and more volunteers increased.

By March 1917 the Red Cross had applied to the workhouse committee to increase the number of beds at Penlan Road. The committee recommended that the whole of the so called "new block" of buildings, including the kitchen and adjacent rooms, together with the use of the laundry for three days a week, should be given over to the Red Cross. The Red Cross Hospital in Carmarthen began with 40 but that had increased to 110 by the end of the War. There were similar increases in the number of beds at the other auxiliary hospitals at Llandeilo and Llandovery and in August 1918 a new 40-bed hospital at Dolygarreg was due to open. By the end of January 1919 no more patients were being accepted at Penlan Road and the building was to be put in order, ready for the Guardians of the workhouse to take it over once again as soon as possible.

Group of wounded soldiers outside Carmarthen Red Cross Hospital wearing Hospital Blues.
The soldiers cap badges reveal them to come from various regiments including the
Lancashire Fusiliers, Royal Artillery and London Rifle Brigade.
Nurse Dulcie Peel is in the centre of the group.

VADs

When the VADs were formed it was decided volunteers, both men and women, should wear a uniform. The women's nursing uniform was a pale blue dress of one length from neck to ankle, sufficiently full that it could be worn over an ordinary dress, if need be. Buttoned at the front with a neck band on which to fasten a white collar, which could be a stiff, shaped, stand-up "Sister Victoria" pattern, or a soft turned-down collar. Until 1915 the cap was a "Sister Dora" type, with a three inch hem turned over at the front, which was square, the other part being rounded with a tape for drawing it up. From 1915 onward the headdress was a rectangle of white, unstarched cambric or linen. Placed centrally on the head, the short front edge was worn straight across the forehead and the two corners brought straight around the back of the head and fastened with a safety pin over the folds, which hung down the back of the neck. The nurses also wore white linen over-sleeves, fifteen inches long, fastened at the cuff with one button and elastic at the elbow, a white linen apron with the Red Cross emblem on the bib, with a large square pocket on both sides. It had a two inch waistband and cross-over straps at the back, all fastened with buttons. In addition a starched white linen belt, two and half inches wide, was worn over the apron. Ordinary black boots and stockings completed the uniform.

Nurses at the Red Cross Hospital Carmarthen.

All members of the VAD were trained in first aid and home nursing. The women, who were the majority of the volunteers, were also trained in hygiene by approved medics and took classes in cookery. Most work was voluntary but some roles, such as that of cook, were paid a wage. The duties experienced by VADs could be cleaning, scrubbing and dusting, setting trays, cooking breakfasts, lighting fires and boiling up coppers full of washing. They also helped to dress, undress and wash the men in their care. This would have been difficult for a young lady who would normally be chaperoned when with a man who was not a relative, let alone performing such an intimate task. Each VAD unit would take it in turns to serve at their local hospital for a given period.

Proficiency badges were awarded to Red Cross VAD members. These were granted for a third examination success in First aid, home nursing, or hygiene and sanitation examinations, provided 12 months had elapsed since the previous exam. They were also awarded for an advanced certificate or two certificates in an individual subject. Bars were granted to each of the three proficiency badges, or for the fourth and subsequent success in any one subject. One year's war service was signified by a bar of 2½ inch long, ¼ inch wide, red lace, worn horizontally on the left forearm. For two and three year service a further bar was added ¼ inch below the last one. For four year service a 4 inch long bar of ½ inch wide blue and white herringbone braid, also worn on left forearm, replaced the previous war service bars. VADs who qualified for the position of Assistant Nurse were permitted to wear a blue stripe on the right sleeve below the shoulder, in addition to the war service stripes on the left sleeve, and a letter 'A' on the bib of the apron above the Red Cross. In 1920 the Red Cross War Medal was awarded to members of the Red Cross or its VAD who served between 4th August, 1914 and 31st December, 1919 and whose unpaid service was more than 1,000 hours.

RED CROSS NURSES

Many local women volunteered to work part-time in the auxiliary hospitals and local doctors also volunteered. The nurses from Laugharne were mainly young, single women from the middle and upper classes, who were able to give their time freely, but more importantly for them it would have been a matter of patriotic duty. Many may also have had a more personal reason, because their own brothers were serving at the front. Of the nurses who came from Laugharne, five had brothers who were killed in action.

The need for nurses became more urgent as the war continued, and frequent appeals went out for more women to come forward, for both military and auxiliary hospitals at home and abroad. During the last 18 months of the war the Red Cross reported a falling off in volunteers, due to women being offered more well-paid posts in many different walks of life, whereas the Red Cross work was voluntary and personal expenses were high. That pattern can be seen in the young women volunteers from Laugharne. Several volunteered for nursing in 1914 and 1915, but only three in 1917/1918, whereas about a dozen young women from Laugharne joined the WAACs from 1917 onwards when good wages for a variety of jobs were not generally available to women, plus accommodation and rations were on offer. This was an important consideration when some foods were becoming harder to obtain towards the end of the war.

The first three women from Laugharne to volunteer at the Red Cross Hospital in Carmarthen were Miss Constance David, Miss May David and Miss Emily Jones, who all registered on the same date, the 29th December, 1914. Constance was the oldest of Laugharne's nurses. Born in 1870 in Laugharne, she had previously been a companion to a lady in Bristol and may have had some home nursing experience as a result. When she volunteered she was living at the Cors. Her family had previously lived at the Pynes in King Street. According to her VAD card on the Red Cross website, she served as a nurse for a total of about 1,000 hours. In May 1915 she was reported as undertaking night duty at the hospital. Previously in February that year, Constance had been elected by the County Council, to the management of

Left to Right: May David, Dulcie Peel, Emily Jones and an unnamed Red Cross Nurse.

Whitland Intermediate School, which served the district. She was described as a capable lady and was very active in many aspects of community life, including serving on the Laugharne Belgian Refugee Committee.

May David was born in Laugharne in 1895, and lived at Minerva House in King Street with her parents, brothers and sisters. May served at the Highland Moors Red Cross Hospital in Llandrindod Wells as well as in Carmarthen for a total of 3,230 hours, as both nurse and cook and was awarded one war service bar. Described in a newspaper report as 'an active and efficient member of the Red Cross', she was also involved in providing Christmas parcels for Laugharne 'boys' on active service and raising funds to repair the local school.

Emily Jones was born in Laugharne in 1890, her family lived in Broadway and she became Governess to the Peel family, who lived at Fernhill. She served as a nurse at the Red Cross Hospital in Carmarthen for a total of 3,336 hours, the greatest number of hours of any of Laugharne's volunteers, and she, too, was awarded one war service bar.

On 14th June, 1915 Mrs Janet Margretta Ravenscroft Starke (nee David) also volunteered, working at both the Red Cross Hospital in Llandrindod Wells and later at Carmarthen. Born in 1888 in Laugharne, she was the older sister of May David who had similarly volunteered in Llandrindod Wells and they may have served together at both hospitals. Gretta as she was known, had previously worked as a nurse in a private nursing home in Llandrindod Wells

Emily Jones standing outside Fernhill.

*Emily Jones front right, Dulcie Peel back right
and two unknown nurses.*

and therefore had some experience. She volunteered as nurse and cook and served a total of 2,100 hours. In July 1918 she married James Llewellyn Ravenscroft Starke of Laugharne Castle. Although the wedding took place in Westminster, Laugharne celebrated the occasion by hanging out flags and banners around the town and the bells of St Martin's 'chimed forth their merry peals'.

From 1st December, 1917 Miss Dulcie Peel began volunteering at Carmarthen Red Cross Hospital as a kitchen orderly and nurse. The youngest of the nurses from the Township, she was born in Laugharne on 1st January, 1901 and was only 16 when she began working at the hospital, where she served a total of 582 hours. Her family lived at Fernhill and employed Emily Jones as their Governess. It may have been the example set by Emily that inspired Dulcie to volunteer, although Dulcie also contributed to a number of good causes together, as we have seen, with her mother, Mrs Minnie Peel, from the very outbreak of the war, including raising funds for the sick and wounded, the Belgian refugees and the Red Cross and she also participated in the many entertainments and social functions organised in the town.

The last of Laugharne's nurses to volunteer at Carmarthen was Miss Eileen Mordaunt-Smith on 18th February, 1918. Born in Rugby in 1897, her family moved to live at Milton Bank. She served as Nurse, ward and kitchen orderly at Carmarthen Red Cross Hospital for a total of 532 hours. Like many in Laugharne, her whole family were involved in the war effort in some way or another. Two of Eileen's brothers saw service, one in the army, the other the navy. Her step-father Major William Murray Matthew also served in France and her mother Mrs Ethel Matthew was secretary of the Soldier & Sailors Families Association, raising funds and making garments for families in need.

Most Red Cross volunteers signed up for home service and were not sent abroad, the majority remaining in the UK. However from 1915 onwards, after a suitable training period, some were sent to the front line to assist the professional nursing staff there. One of Laugharne's Red Cross nurses who went to France was Ruth Laugharne Allen. Born in Lancashire in 1892, she lived in Liverpool with her parents and brothers and in 1911 was studying at Art College. The family kept a house in Liverpool and came to Laugharne from time to time, where they resided at Gosport House for long periods. Ruth first served at an auxiliary hospital in Liverpool for 10 months before going to France in January 1917. Her record shows she was nursing in No 7 Stationary Hospital in Boulogne for two years, until 28th January, 1919. She was paid £20 plus a field allowance and awarded an efficiency stripe (a scarlet stripe worn on the right sleeve below the shoulder) on 4th April, 1918.

Although the majority of Laugharne's VAD nurses had no professional nursing qualifications which would be recognised today, there were some young women from Laugharne who were registered nurses and followed a professional career. One of these, who also saw service abroad, was Miss Maud Todman. One of 10 children, she was born in Laugharne in 1889. Her family had lived in Victoria Street, but by 1911 they had moved away to live in Willesden and Maud began her training as a probationary nurse at the West Ham Infirmary, Whipps Cross Road in Leytonstone. She progressed in her career to become a Sister. On 14th November, 1914 she enlisted with the Queen Alexandra's Imperial Military Nursing Service (QAIMS) and served throughout the war until May 1919. After first serving for a year in England, she was sent to Salonika, arriving there on 1st February 1916, where she remained for just over 2 years until 10th April, 1918, after which she nursed at the 29th General Hospital.

The war in Salonika began in October 1915 in an attempt by the allies to aid Serbia against attack by Bulgaria. The allied army dug in and there was limited fighting until 1918 when an allied offensive broke the Bulgarian defences and an armistice was signed on 29th September, 1918. As well as battle casualties, the main cause of hospital admissions in Salonika was malaria. There were 160,000 cases, including medical staff, in the 3 years that the army was there. One QAIMS nurse in Salonika, who had previously nursed at Carmarthen Infirmary, Miss Frances Brace, contracted malaria and was evacuated to a hospital in Malta where, sadly, she died in September 1916. On arriving back in England, Maud was posted to the King George V Hospital in Dublin until 1919. This hospital specialised in neurological cases which had been identified as the result of soldier's experiences during the war.

In a despatch from Lieutenant General G.F. Milne, Commander-in-Chief, British Salonika Force, dated 25th March 1918, Maud was mentioned among those recommended for gallant conduct and distinguished services. The list was published in the London Gazette on 11th June. Maud was then awarded the Royal Red Cross (2nd class) and was decorated by the King at Buckingham Palace on 10th December 1919. This award had been established in 1883 by Queen Victoria and was awarded for exceptional service in military nursing, either in the performance of duties or for an exceptional act of bravery. We do not know the details leading to Maud's decoration but her service records from the National Archives show, in a report signed by the Matron at the hospital in Salonika and the Colonel at the base, that she was a 'good ward sister, kind and attentive to her patients and a good disciplinarian.'

Group of Military nurses leaving Buckingham Palace after receiving the Royal Red Cross.

Although the Todman family had left Laugharne some years earlier, they were still remembered and their contribution to the war was acknowledged in *The Welshman* in June 1918 when it was reported that three Todman brothers were serving the King, two in the army and one in the Royal Field Artillery and three sisters also, including Maud, but also Margery (employed in the Ministry of Munitions) and Thomasina (a nurse in a London military hospital). Thomasina had enrolled for training as a midwife in October 1911. She appears on the Midwives Roll for 1915 and 1920 practising midwifery in Cornwall, but details of her war-time service are not known.

Another young local woman who was a registered nurse and saw service abroad was Penelope Davies. Born in 1887 at Rogers Well, Llansadurnen, to Lewis and Margaret Davies, Penelope began her nursing career in February 1909 at Swansea General Hospital, completing her training as a staff nurse three years later. She then went to the London Cancer Hospital in Fulham Road for a year. In March 1913 she became a sister at the Swansea General Eye Hospital. In May 1916 she joined the Queen Alexandra's Imperial Military Nursing Service. Just over a year later on 26th June, 1917 she embarked for Bombay for her onward journey to Basra in Mesopotamia (now Iraq), where she arrived on 7th July. Her final destination was No 32 British General Hospital in Amara.

A typical road in Mesopotamia.

River Tigris at Amara.

		Marriage Solemnized at The Military Church, Amarah, Mesopotamia.					37

When Married.		Names of Parties.		Age.	Condition.	Rank or Profession.	Residence at the time of Marriage.	Father's name and surname.
Month.	Year.	Christian.	Surname.					
December	1919	George	Shanks	35	Bachelor	Physician (Capt.I.M.S.)	21 I.G.H.,Amarah	James Charles Shanks.Physician
		Penelope	Davies	32	Spinster	----	21 I.G.H.,Amarah	Lewis Davies (deceased). Minister

By Banns or Licence.	Signature of the Parties.	Signature of two or more Witnesses present.	Signature by whom Married.
Banns and by permission of the Inspector General of Communications and the Principal Chaplain M.E.F.	George Shanks Penelope Davies	T.P.Lloyd,Capt. A.D.M.S. E.P.C.Rutter, ?.A.I.M.N.S.R.	Chas.J.Crabtree,C.F. Chaplain i/c Military Church, Amarah. 666

I hereby certify that the above is a true extract from the Register of Marriages kept at the office of the Senior Chaplain,C.of E.,Mesopotamian Expeditionary Force. Dated this 24th day of December 1919.

Marriage certificate of Penelope Davies and George Shanks.

Conditions in Mesopotamia were very poor and many hospital admissions were for disease and sickness. The climate was one of extremes: very hot in summer and bitterly cold in winter. The landscape was either desert or marshland and getting around was difficult, due to the lack of proper roads. Sick or wounded men would often have to be taken long distances for medical attention. On her demobilisation on 5th December, 1919 her testimonial stated that 'her work in the ward has been exceptionally good and she has proved herself a capable charge Sister'. While in Mesopotamia, Penelope met a Canadian doctor, George Shanks, who also served in the hospital and they were married at the Military Church in Amara on 17th December, 1919. George and Penelope later moved to Vancouver, Canada.

During the First World War and in the immediate post-war years, as nursing was increasingly seen as a suitable occupation for single women, due in part to the regard in which nurses were held during the war, but also as an alternative to domestic service, more young women from Laugharne took up nursing. However, little is known about when and where they nursed.

One of these young ladies was Mary Josephine Thomas, born in 1894 to Samuel and Margaret Thomas of Lorenzo, Gosport Street. The 1911 census shows her as a dressmaker's apprentice, then aged 17. She went on to train as a nurse and became a sister at the St Pancras Infirmary, Highgate. Her younger sister, Ada Jane, born in 1901, followed in her footsteps and also became a sister in the City of London District Hospital, which was used as a military hospital during the First World War.

Maria Tucker also became a nurse. Born in 1891 to John and Sarah Tucker, by 1911 she lived in Clifton Street, with her brother Benjamin and widowed mother. She nursed at the 3rd Northern General Hospital, Sheffield, which was a base hospital in the First World War.

Mary Josephine Thomas.

Staff at St Pancras Infirmary.

Nurse Maria Tucker seated left.

FUND-RAISING AND COMMUNITY SUPPORT

Although the Red Cross and St John's organisations had prepared well, they needed to raise funds for more equipment and to maintain the temporary hospital buildings they had acquired and so appeals went out as soon as war was declared. Local fund-raising committees were set up all over the country and in Laugharne such a committee was established by the third week of August 1914. Mr M. Williams of Ashcombe House was elected the Secretary of the Red Cross Fund for the district and Commander Thomas Brayshay of The Glen as Treasurer. A house to house collection was organised straight away.

One month later Mrs Fanny Brayshay of The Glen was elected Honorary Treasurer in place of her son, as he was called up on active service. She remained in this post for the rest of the war.

Local newspapers regularly reported on the sums of money collected or raised through events organised by the Laugharne committee, and the local community were very generous in their support, as the following examples show. At the end of October 1914 Mrs Brayshay reported a recent collection had raised £88. One year later on 21st and 22nd October, 1915 a sale in Laugharne realised between £300 and £400. The monthly report of sub-scriptions received for May 1917 were typical and included £3 from Mrs Brayshay, £50 from Mr & Mrs Morgan Jones, Llanmiloe, £42 7s 0d from a collection in Eglwys Cymin, Pendine and Marros, £2 17s 6d from Mrs Thomas,

Laugharne Vicarage, and £242 10s 0d from Laugharne sales committee. In August 1917 a concert by the Ogmore Vale Concert Party in the grounds of Laugharne Castle made over £50 for the Red Cross and Carmarthen Infirmary. In addition there were other gifts made to the Red Cross Hospital in the form of venison, rabbits, cigarettes, cakes, vegetables, fruit and magazines. Among those who contributed such items were Constance David, May David, Mrs Anne Stark and Mr Herbert Eccles of Broadway Mansion.

In addition to fund-raising, the Red Cross encouraged the setting up of War Hospital Supply Depots and work parties, to be organised by individuals, throughout the UK. These were set up to supply bandages, nightshirts, bed jackets and other garments for patients. There were two depots in Laugharne. One was organised by Mrs Mary Bolton at Elm House (Registration number 5237) and one by Miss Alice Cunningham at Mapsland (Registration number 5781). The fee for registering a work party was 2/6d, regardless of the number of workers and each party was assigned a registration number. They were each sent a small Red Cross flag with their registration number on and labels for the despatch of their supplies to the central stores depot, together with information about hospitals' requirements. Work parties were supplied with a pattern book for them to follow, which included patterns for sewn garments, knitted garments and bandages. Nearly all garments were hand-made by groups and individuals, often paying for the materials out of their own pockets. Without them supplies of dressings and garments for many hospitals would have been non-existent.

Nurses on recreation at Sheffield Hospital.

As has been seen, even the children in Laugharne were not excluded from trying to bring some comfort to wounded soldiers. Many of the older girls were involved in sewing and knitting garments and in April and May 1915 *The Welshman* reported that through the initiative of Mrs Lynham, The Cottage, several children gathered large quantities of primroses, which were forwarded to various hospitals treating wounded soldiers and were dispatched at their own expense. These were so much appreciated that a message of thanks was sent in the form of a picture postcard, showing a group of men on a balcony, who were the grateful recipients of the flowers. Those children mentioned were Winnie Jones, Amy Harries, Lizzie Thomas and Evan Thomas.

EGGS FOR THE WOUNDED

One of the earliest campaigns of the war was the National Egg Collection for wounded soldiers, launched in November 1914. An appeal was placed in *The Carmarthen Journal* on 2nd July, 1915 for anyone who would distribute leaflets, organise collections of new laid eggs in their district or collect cash for the purchase of eggs, from those unable to give eggs. The eggs would be dispatched to a local receiving centre for which there was no charge for carriage, using the special labels supplied on application.

The eggs were sent to base hospitals in France and throughout the United Kingdom. Although there was no official organiser in Laugharne until April 1917, in September 1915 it was learned that the Red Cross Hospital in Carmarthen was suffering from an egg shortage. As noted in an earlier chapter, in just one day the children of Laugharne School managed to collect 200 eggs and, as was customary, each egg bore the name of the donor. A few days later, Miss Elizabeth John of Wooford, age 9, received a letter of thanks from Sergeant C. Davies Regimental No 15214 of the 4th South Wales Borderers, who was at the Red Cross Hospital in Penlan Road, recovering from wounds he had received in the Dardanelles on 21st August. He wrote:

> I herewith enclose a little verse if you would care to add it to your little book of autographs you may do so, as your name was written on the egg I had for breakfast:
>
> > Then take with rejoicing from Jesus at once,
> > The life everlasting he gives,
> > And know with assurance thou never can'st die,
> > Since Jesus thy righteousness lives.

In Laugharne the local organiser for egg collection in the district was Mr Reginald Fitzgerald Ravenscroft Starke of Laugharne Castle. Each week *The Welshman* reported on the number of eggs donated and the amount of money collected. Although the number of eggs and the amount of money raised fell off towards the end of the war, in February 1918 it was reported that in the last few months the sum of £20. 8s. 0d. had been forwarded and that a total of 4,397 eggs had been donated. This campaign finally closed on 31st March, 1919 by which time over 41 million eggs had been collected nationwide, and a few thousand of those had come from Laugharne!

In June 1915 an appeal was placed in *The Welshman* newspaper for owners of motor cars to lend their cars to take wounded soldiers for drives on one afternoon a week. This was already being done in England. Within a couple of weeks a party of wounded soldiers, from the Carmarthen Red Cross hospital, were taken to Pendine where they were entertained by residents and visitors, including Mr Morgan Jones of Llanmiloe, and catered for by the proprietor of the Beach Hotel, Mr Ebsworth.

This was the first of several outings reported in the local papers, usually to Pendine, with refreshments being taken at the Beach Hotel. *The Welshman* of 9th August, 1918 gave a very full account of a party of wounded soldiers from Carmarthen who came to Laugharne on 31st July, when the streets were decorated with flags and banners to greet them.

> The trip was organised by Mr C. Chapman of Carmarthen who a short time ago wrote to Mr Tyler stating he would like to take the soldiers for an outing to Laugharne. The matter was brought before the Welcome Fund committee (which had been formed in the latter part of 1917) who agreed to entertain them and a committee of ladies were appointed consisting of Mrs Matthew and Miss Eileen Mordaunt-Smith of Milton Bank, Mrs Peel and Miss Dulcie Peel of Fernhill, Mrs S. David and Mai

Llanmiloe House, home of Mr Morgan Jones.

Pendine showing the Beach Hotel to the right of the slipway

David of Minerva, Mrs Wilson, The Corse, & Miss E. Falkener, Glanymor. A house to house collection was organised and residents generously responded in cash and kind. The party arrived in a motor charabanc about 3pm and were received at the Town Hall. The Portreeve welcomed the party and a start was made at the Grist where the ancient cross was inspected. A halt was made at Island House where Colonel and Mrs Congreve kindly presented each with a quantity of cigarettes and fruit. Returning to the schools at 4.30pm a sumptuous tea was partaken of. After tea the Castle was visited by kind permission of Mrs Starke and a walk through the grounds was led by Mr Tyler and others. Then a walk over the Cliff and a return to the schools where luncheon was partaken of consisting of ham and other sandwiches, milk, lemonade etc. A large quantity of cigars and cigarettes given by the tradespeople were distributed. At this juncture Mrs Evans, Ashleigh (the aged and respected aunt of the first Welsh VC, Sergeant Fuller) presented each man with a silver sixpence as a souvenir of the visit, stating that no one should say our brave soldiers had left Laugharne penniless. Mr Chapman thanked everyone for the great kindness shown. On their return to Carmarthen at the entrance to The Glen the car was stopped when Mrs Brayshay and Miss Brayshay presented the party with fruit and a book to each man."

Mr Herbert Eccles house at Broadway.

The Carmarthen Weekly Reporter of 30th August, 1918 wrote of a party of wounded soldiers being entertained by Mr and Mrs Jones of Llanmiloe, having a very enjoyable day. And again on 27th September, 1918 soldiers were 'hospitably entertained by the genial squire of Broadway', Mr Herbert Eccles.

As the weather turned more autumnal and the war entered its final months, these were the last outings by wounded soldiers to the Laugharne area from the Red Cross Hospital in Carmarthen. The remaining soldiers once recovered, were discharged and the hospital finally closed its doors in January 1919.

Chapter 7

The Aftermath

In an earlier chapter, it was shown how Laugharne's annual carnival was affected by wartime and how even everyday life, such as theatre and cinema entertainment, was dominated by the war. And the momentum of that continued for some time after. The image below was taken after the war had ended. The float is now being drawn by a horse instead of the donkey but the theme appears to be celebration of the Union – with Britannia standing, surrounded by representatives of the nations of the United Kingdom.

A triumphant post-victory carnival display.

The war had ended, victory had been finally achieved and peace was being celebrated, but the effects of that brutal campaign continued to be felt – and would be for generations to come.

More than 400 men and women with connections to Laugharne had donned uniforms to serve in the war and many more had served on the Home Front, such as in munitions factories and in many other essential roles. 35 of them are commemorated on the war memorial and these are the fallen who had been residents of Laugharne – although people here would have been aware of more losses than that number, for example, folk who had left the area within living memory to seek employment elsewhere. At the county level, altogether nearly 2,000 servicemen and women from across Carmarthenshire had died in the war and so it is unsurprising that uppermost in the minds of residents were plans to honour those who had paid that highest sacrifice.

MEMORIALS

There can be little as thought-provoking, or more poignant, than to spend some minutes looking at the names on a First World War memorial. One can look at the names and see patterns: perhaps a good few of the men served in the same regiment or unit. Perhaps there are surnames the same, which look likely to have been relatives. If the memorial carries dates, perhaps there are clusters in the timings of the losses, reflecting men who fought and died together. All of these things are visible on memorials across the UK, and they all tell a story. Almost every town, village and hamlet has one and they even appear in workplaces, such as the wonderfully evocative memorial at Paddington Station in London, the beautiful roll of honour in the postal sorting office in Pontypridd, and there are similar tributes in many schools and colleges. Only a few, very few, communities have no such memorial since that particular community lost none of its men. These are rare places indeed. They are known as 'thankful villages', and they had a lot to be thankful for. There are just 52 civil parishes in England and Wales which were 'thankful' for having no losses in the war, and a pitiably low three of these are in Wales: Herbrandston in Pembrokeshire, Llanfihangel y Creuddyn in Ceredigion, and Colwinston in the Vale of Glamorgan. Laugharne, therefore, cherishes its war memorials in common with all communities where they are sited.

On a grander scale, there are the national memorials to the fallen. The best known of these is the Cenotaph in Whitehall, London, which was initially a wood and plaster construction intended only for the first anniversary of the

Armistice in 1919. At its unveiling the base of the monument was spontaneously covered in wreaths to the dead and missing from the Great War. Such was the extent of public enthusiasm for the construction it was decided that the Cenotaph should become a permanent and lasting memorial and it pointed the way for commemorative memorials across the country, and possibly the world. If one remembers that families of the lost servicemen had no easily accessible grave on which to focus their mourning, and there were almost 990,000 British military deaths in the conflict, then it is very clear indeed why these memorials were so very important in communities – they were essential.

As the war was far more protracted than anyone, expert or otherwise, predicted at the outset, it is not surprising that some individual memorials to lost sons or family members were erected during the war itself. They are among the first such memorials and in St Martin's church in Laugharne there are a number of these. For example, Eric Western Wilson, the first Laugharne soldier to lose his life, has a beautiful brass memorial in the church, erected by his family. Lieutenant Wilson, sadly, shares his memorial plaque with his uncle, Lt Commander Thomas Morgan David, who died in the sinking of HMS *Hawke* in the North Sea on October 15th, 1914.

Also on the church walls is another double memorial: to the popular local young men, brothers John Ritso Nelson Bolton and Stuart Bladen Nelson Bolton, killed in 1915 and 1916 respectively.

The first of these privately erected memorials to be installed in St Martin's was that of Lionel St George Mordaunt-Smith, the eldest son of the late Mordaunt K Mordaunt-Smith and Mrs Mathew of Milton Bank. It was installed in December 1917.

It is not at all unusual for a serviceman to be commemorated on more than one memorial. For example, those memorials located in schools, colleges or workplaces carry names that will certainly be included on their home community's memorial, too. Locally, the memorial tablet at Bwlchnewydd Chapel (unveiled in June 1919 and finely executed by Mr Owen Williams and Brothers, sculptors, of Laugharne) carries the names of men who were associated with that place of worship:

Gwyn Thomas, Post Office, St Clears
William James, saddler, St Clears
David T John, Halfpenny Furze, Laugharne
Llew H Evans, Craesland, Laugharne
Richard Edwards, Morfa Bach, Laugharne
John J John, Halfpenny Furze, Laugharne

The Bolton brothers double memorial, St Martin's Church.

2nd Lt. Mordaunt Smith: the first of numerous Great War memorials in Laugharne.

The four Laugharne men named above are also recorded on the memorial in St Martin's and at the Hall. As every community would have wished to include all men associated with that specific location, there are overlaps, too, in the names included on the marble monument in Llanddowror church. Among them are David T John and John J John – who are therefore commemorated in all three communities.

In Laugharne itself, the agreement that the Township's memorial to the fallen would be in the shape of a community hall was made at a public meeting held on 1st May, 1920. It was clearly a democratic decision since, according to *The Carmarthen Journal*, present at the meeting were:

> …the residents of full age of the township of Laugharne and the parishes of Laugharne, Llansadurnen and Llandawke in the county of Carmarthen…

The meeting (sadly the number of attendees is not recorded) was held at the school and it was here that:

> …resolutions were duly passed (i) to erect a public hall as a memorial to those members of His Majesty's services inhabitants of the said Township and parishes who fell in the Great War 1914 to 1918 (ii) that the said hall should be used solely for the following purposes namely to provide a suitable meeting place for meetings providing for good fellowship and social well-being and for indoor recreation…

This was obviously a major decision and, no doubt, it was not taken lightly, with much discussion taking place about sculptures, marble tablets, or obelisk type memorials chosen by other communities. So the decision on the type of memorial was taken by the Township as a whole and it was done within 18 months of the Armistice. However, that was clearly the easy part! Then the more challenging tasks had to be faced: forming a committee to oversee the project, finding a suitably located plot of land of the right size, and – all important – funding the purchase of the land and the construction of the building itself. This was obviously a lengthy and challenging process since it was over five years later, on 14th November, 1925, that an indenture was drafted and signed which legally confirmed the sale of a parcel of land from Thomas Edmunds of East Hill Farm, to the Trustees of the War Memorial Hall. The plot was purchased for £25. The indenture also helpfully agreed that, in perpetuity:

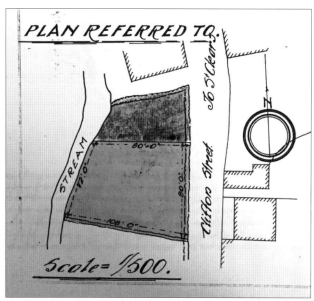

*The plan of the land sold by Farmer Thomas Edmunds
to be the site of the Memorial Hall.*

servants and workmen could pass and re-pass over [an adjacent area of land] for the purpose of hauling to the back of the said hall material for building or coal for heating... Or for any similar purpose.

The indenture was signed by Thomas Edmunds (as the vendor) and by Hubert Richard Griffith and Frederick Norman Jones (as Trustees of the Memorial Hall) and it was witnessed by Mr Tyler, Headmaster, of Osborne House.

As momentous as this purchase was – the project was at last on its way – it had, in effect, already been launched! The foundation stone for the Memorial Hall had already been laid, with great ceremony, some five months *before* the land was legally purchased! And the reasons for this are long forgotten!

The laying of the foundation stone ceremony was a major event in the Township and was reported in detail in *The Carmarthen Journal*. It was held on Friday afternoon, June 5th, 1925. A large gathering was present to witness Miss Norah Mond perform the laying of the foundation stone which was incised simply:

Laugharne War Memorial
This stone was laid by
Miss Norah Mond
5th June 1925

Who was Miss Norah Mond? Not a local name. She was the 20 year-old daughter of the sitting MP for Carmarthen, Sir Alfred Mond. A wealthy industrialist, he served as MP for Carmarthen for a short spell from 1924 to 1928, initially as a Liberal, but he switched parties to become a Conservative after falling out with David Lloyd George. It is not recorded how the choice of VIP to lay the stone was regarded among Laugharne folk but, such was the social deference to 'the gentry' as it was in those days that it was probably not questioned at all.

The architect of the hall, Mr WSP Cottrell, from Carmarthen, was present, and he said it was a very proud moment for him to be 'associated in some humble way with the ceremony'. Mr W Jones, the contractor, presented Miss Mond with a silver trowel, suitably inscribed, with which she performed the ceremony, remarking "I declare this stone well and truly laid." Other speeches followed from Commander Brayshay (of the Glen) representing the Navy, General St John of Llanddowror representing the Army, and Reverend EW Edwards and Reverend WT Watson representing the churches. *The Journal* goes on to report that:

> Mr W Clarke Griffiths, on behalf of the War Memorial Committee, pro-posed a hearty vote of thanks to Miss Mond for coming there that day. It was evident to all present that the committee had, after consideration and labour, made an excellent beginning to carry out the decision of a public meeting to erect a much-needed hall to the memory of their gallant sons who nobly laid down their lives in the great cause of freedom and liberty. The only regret was that lack of means prevented them from carrying out the full project in its entirety.

Mr Griffiths was hinting in his speech that the process was costly and still had a long way to go.

The work on the Hall progressed and it eventually opened on Wednesday, 17th March, 1926. Once again, the good and the great, and the townsfolk as a whole, rose to the occasion and a grand ceremony was held at 3.00pm. A full and detailed account appeared in *The Welshman* on 26th March, 1926 which recounted the lengthy speeches in enormous detail! The formal opening was due to be performed by a distinguished soldier with local forebears, Major Rowland Lewis, DSO, but some unavoidable circumstance prevented his attendance and, instead, the opening duty was undertaken by Commander Brayshay. The report in the newspaper describes the building as:

Situated on the right hand side of the Township as one enters from the direction of St Clears, the hall is stone built with a grey Caernarfon slated roof. The external walls are cemented, and although perfectly plain, the external elevations are quite pleasing. The interior has been carefully planned, and treated in every way, with seating capacity for 500. It is perfectly clear that the architect has quite obtained his objective – to erect a commodious, useful and substantial hall, with no thought for any unnecessary superficial decoration. The whole building rests nicely in harmony with its ancient, time-coloured surroundings. A memorial tablet, designed by the Hon. Architect, and erected by Mr A.M. Lewis, monumental mason, Carmarthen, has been placed in the main external wall, and this has quite put the necessary finish to the whole scheme.

However, despite the triumph of arriving at the official opening day, there is a hint of disquiet in the speech by the Portreeve, Benjamin Tucker:

Despite a certain amount of opposition, the committee never lost heart, because they felt they were on the right track. There were hundreds of towns and parishes where similar halls were built to the memory of the fallen in the Great War, so that Laugharne were not alone in their endeavour. The opposition had been surmounted, thanks to the sacrifices made by the inhabitants of the township and district.

A financial statement was presented by the Hon. Treasurer, Mr George Wilkins, which revealed that the hall had cost £1,358 14 shillings and 6d and that there was an outstanding debt of £200. The opening ceremony was followed by an evening concert under the presidency of the vicar, Rev. E.W. Edwards.

The Hall, then as now, carried a memorial to the men; 35 of whom are commemorated there and on a tablet in St Martin's Church. These days, as local people and visitors know, another memorial bearing the names (together with the addition of the names of the fallen from the Second World War) has been installed at the side of the Hall and, today, this is the site of annual commemorations on Remembrance Sunday. The current memorial also has a commemorative paving stone recording William Fuller's award of the Victoria Cross, the first to a Welsh soldier in the Great War.

As a footnote, it is worth noting that, despite the old hall suffering subsidence and being replaced with the hall the Township has today, the original foundation stone, laid by Miss Mond, is still there. Not easily visible, perhaps, but there it is, tucked away on the bottom left side of the low wall alongside the current memorial.

The Memorial Hall, pictured not long before its demolition.

*The current memorial alongside the Hall,
with the VC commemorative stone in front.*

The well-worn but original Hall foundation stone laid in 1925.

LONG TERM EFFECTS

Putting up memorials may have helped people to express their grief but, of course, it did not extinguish it. Memories continued to haunt people.

Seven years after the war ended Mr Tyler and his senior pupils compiled a hand-written book (copies of which are still in print and on sale) about Laugharne's history in which he wrote:

> 'In the early days of the Great War, the young men of Laugharne voluntarily rallied to the ranks of the Army and Navy in large numbers. By the termination of hostilities thirty-five had laid down their lives in the great cause of Freedom and Liberty'.

And here, too, they recorded the names of those who had been killed.

Clearly Mr Tyler was still moved by the sacrifices made by local people and in Kitty John's memory the old Headmaster, still living in Osborne House, on King Street would on every Victory Day thereafter hang out flags to commemorate the end of the war.

The book written by Laugharne's school-children.

After a due period of mourning people were expected to 'get over it' and 'get on with living'. And most outwardly appeared to do so. Nevertheless there were lasting effects. For example, throughout his life if ever a photo or memento of William Constable appeared, his younger brother, Philip, would shed a tear. Memories remained long with the survivors and with relatives – and those memories still hurt.

Those who did return from the war often returned profoundly affected by their experiences. For most, like Charley Lewis, those experiences had been so horrific that they simply could not talk about it, and so we have no real knowledge of its effects.

Post Traumatic Stress Disorder (PTSD) has only recently been officially recognised (it was in 1980 that the American Psychiatric Association added the condition to its diagnostic manual) yet it existed throughout time – in 1917, the term 'shell shock' was coined by a Medical Officer, Dr Charles Myers. Similarly, it was not uncommon for soldiers to be hospitalised for periods suffering from 'Neurasthenia', a state of mental exhaustion associated with emotional disturbance. The war, no surprise, was traumatic, shocking and emotionally disturbing. But soldiers suffering from stress, however labelled, were needed urgently at the Front. It was therefore pretty common in the First World War for someone suffering from the condition to be told to 'stiffen up'

185

– the fortunate men might have got a week's sick-leave, but imagine the additional stress of returning to the front line after a week's safety in a clean bed. Similarly, many of those at home had to cope with the loss of a loved one. Some might have been able to do so, but for many the effects had been so mind-numbing that they could not fully settle down.

After the War, Gwynne Tucker recalled that tramps:

> "Gentlemen of the Road" frequently passed through the town..., going from one known place of overnight refuge to another ... invariably clad in several ragged raincoats or overcoats and carrying a bundle of belongings. One poor man was known as 'Him Hom' for always he intoned those two syllables to the same two notes as he walked through the town.

It is not known how many ex-soldiers turned to this roaming way of life, unable to settle back into civilian ways as a result of their wartime experiences.

For some, drink numbed the painful memories for years afterwards, but with consequent effects upon their family members. Likewise, but almost invisible in the stories of the war are those who came back with lasting, life-changing injuries, like Thomas John Harry. A doctor recalled that many ex-soldiers, when X-rayed later in their lives, showed shrapnel pieces embedded in their bodies that they had never told anyone about. They 'did not want to cause a fuss'.

Even worse was the longer-term mental damage that so many suffered. The worst cases were shut away in mental institutions, such as the old St David's Hospital in Carmarthen, often cut off from outside contacts. Yet, even for those who could remain at home the effects on their own lives and on their families, too, were enormous. It is usually said that those engaged in the fighting never talked about it once they were home. Yet many suffered. Gwynne Tucker's uncle:

> ...was one of the participants of the ill-fated Dardenelles Campaign and had to run the gauntlet from a hole in the side of the ship, the River Clyde, over a pontoon to the shore, under intense fire from the cliffs above. This he succeeded in doing, only to be hit later and left for three days in No-Man's land after a retreat, from which he survived with the loss of one lung and four ribs. Even this did not invalid him out of the Forces, but left him in indifferent health till he died at under the age of 50.

IMMEDIATE EFFECTS

The end of the war did not suddenly restore everyday life back to pre-war normality. Although the the conflict had ended, shortages, for example of sugar, continued for some time afterwards. In February 1919 the Carmarthen Rural Food Control Committee received an application from Mr Dalton of the Broadway Estate for 7lbs of fine white sugar. The explanation given was that the estate's gamekeeper used his own 'mixture' against rats, the concoction contained arsenic and sugar (to disguise the poison)! Needless to say the committee did not grant the application.

Not all immediate effects of the end of the conflict were miserable. Celebrations continued, and once the lengthy peace negotiations concluded with Treaty of Versailles being signed in June 1919, the Government's 'Peace Committee' outlined a celebration running over four days and on the morning of 19th July, 1919, King George V issued a message to the wounded soldiers and celebrations and marches were held throughout the country. The day was known as the official 'Peace Celebration Day'. Gwynne Tucker recalled at the age of four being shown, through the kitchen window, the Peace bonfire as it was being built on Sir John's Hill and he remembered being taken to see it burning. Also as a reward for their contribution to the war effort, in the summer of 1919, at the King's request, school children were granted an extra week's holiday, this was called "Peace Week", but it may have been more welcomed by the children than the parents!

OTHER LEGACIES

Even today, more than a century after the Great War and several generations on from those directly involved, its effects can be felt upon us, albeit lightly.

Chapter two outlined a number of legislative changes that were made during World War One, often as 'temporary measures' but which have persisted through to today. They included daylight saving time and passport photographs. Whilst rationing and conscription took a long time to be legislated for in World War One, that precedent meant that in future they would be more speedily turned to. Perhaps the biggest gain came with voting rights. If young men were expected to fight and die for their country, then clearly they deserved the right to vote, so in February 1918, the Representation of the People Act 1918 reformed the electoral system in Great Britain and Ireland. It gave the vote to men aged 21 and over, whether or not they owned property, and to women aged 30 and over who owned property above a certain value. It also allowed women aged 21 and over the right to vote in local Government elections. Arguably, the war may have accelerated changes which were already germinating, rather than been the sole cause of them, but the influence of war cannot be denied.

It has been shown that during the war various pressures on labour forces had led to strikes, demands for higher wages and better working conditions and to the strengthening of trade unions. That process was to continue and to grow over the decades that followed the war. The number of women in trade unions had tripled between 1914 and 1918 to more than a million, though their wages remained low such that even by 1931 theirs was still only half that of their male counterparts!

The involvement of so many from all ranks of life, male and female, in the war effort would eventually stir a rising sense of equality among those 'labouring classes'. For the older generation of men, however, nothing had changed. After church on Sundays they would still stroll back along Clifton and King Street to gather at the Mariner's corner for a chat and a smoke and, in Gwynne Tucker's words:

> ...hats or caps were doffed or a forelock touched, and in return a hand was raised royal-like in acknowledgement

as the Daimler of Mr and Mrs Morgan Jones of Llanmilo, or the Napier of Mr Eccles of Broadway Mansion or the car bearing Mrs Peel of Fernhill passed by. The younger generation, however, was beginning to break the mould. When young Dulcie Peel was driven by one day, one of her schoolmates failed to curtsy in the expected manner. The vicar called round on the offender to remind her of her place and its expectations, but the die was cast – society was gradually changing, and involvement in the war effort had accelerated the change.

In July 1914 women represented only 24% of the British work force, half of them in very low-paid domestic service. By the end of the war that figure had risen to 37% and included nearly five million women in industry or commerce. Employment of women in the Civil Service rose from 33,000 in 1911 to 102,000 by 1921. Women were earning higher wages, better conditions and greater independence. The return of men from the war fronts ousted many women from their 'temporary' employment but, for those who needed convincing, women had shown that they could do the 'work of men' and whilst even now, a hundred years later, true equality of employment and pay is still proving a struggle, the gaps have been closing ever since the Great War.

As discussed earlier in this book, on local farms the wartime losses of horses and labour quickened the pace of the mechanisation of farming – and this trend was to accelerate over time. With it came the increased movement of farm-labouring families, displaced from the countryside into urban areas to look for reliable work. Farmers had also begun to form cooperatives to market their produce and purchase resources and that process continued. But the diversion of Britain's industrial workforce to war-related production had, meanwhile, prompted other countries (that had previously imported goods produced in the UK) to manufacture their own, which led to falling demand here and contributed to the long recession that followed the war.

Thus the Great War can be seen from today's perspective to have had a significant impact, not only on the families at home in Laugharne and those directly engaged, but upon almost every aspect of daily life in Britain over the succeeding decades.

Gwynne Tucker, in his own book, *Yesteryear: Laugharne in the inter-war years*, remembers an idealised, happy and contented life in Laugharne in that period, with many busy shops, tradespeople and banks, with entertainments and outings, with continuing traditions such as those of the Corporation. With the simple outlook of a youngster, he doesn't observe long-lasting grief and fatherless children and he makes no mention of the clouds of a further conflict gathering on the horizon. It is to be hoped that our forebears in Laugharne enjoyed the peace for the 20 years it lasted and that while the fallen were duly honoured and remembered with love, that life went on in the Township in much the way it had for many centuries.